More Than *Miracles*

T. C. Christensen filming 17 Miracles

More Than *Miracles*

Extraordinary Stories from

17 Miracles

T. C. Christensen

with Jolene S. Allphin

Deseret Book

Salt Lake City, Utah

Photos on pages ii and 106 courtesy Remember Films.
Photo on page 101 courtesy Daniel K. Adams.

Visit us at DeseretBook.com

Library of Congress Cataloging-in-Publication Data

Christensen, T. C., author.
More than miracles : extraordinary stories from 17 Miracles / T. C. Christensen with Jolene S. Allphin.
p. cm.
Includes bibliographical references.
ISBN 978-1-60907-006-9 (paperbound)
1. 17 miracles (Motion picture)—Production and direction. 2. Savage, Levi, 1820–1910. 3. James G. Willie Emigrating Company—History. I. Allphin, Jolene S. (Jolene Spendlove), 1952– , author. II. Title.
PN1997.2.A133C48 2012
791.43'72—dc23 2012003585

Printed in the United States of America
Malloy Lithographing Incorporated, Ann Arbor, MI

10 9 8 7 6 5 4 3 2 1

Contents

The Making of the Film

T. C. Christensen: As a pimply faced kid in junior high school, I looked in the mirror one day and thought, "What are you ever going to do for a living? You're not smart, you're not good looking, not talented in any way . . . Hmmmmm. I KNOW! That means I have the perfect qualifications for being a movie maker!" One of the results of that decision made many years ago is *17 Miracles.* Whenever a screenplay is based on historical events, viewers of the film frequently want to know if the events being depicted are factual or merely the screenwriter's imaginary version of what might have been. That has certainly been the case with *17 Miracles.* Over the past year or so, since the film was released, I have been asked numerous questions about the story line. Viewers have asked, Were two little girls truly kept from harm while running a gauntlet of agitated rattlesnakes? Did a mysterious man really reveal a stash of dried meat in a cave? Was a beloved daughter, left for dead in a shallow grave, actually brought back to life?

As you will discover in this book, these and the other

miracles depicted in the film are based on the testimonies of those who were involved or who learned of the events from those who witnessed them. Our principal historical adviser in the making of the film was Jolene S. Allphin, who has become a recognized authority on the Willie, Martin, Hunt, and Hodgetts companies and their rescuers. She tried to keep me in line while we were making the movie, and her assistance was invaluable. I am also indebted to her for the documentation provided in this book. In answering the questions, I give commentary on the making of the film and Jolene provides the historical information that is the basis of the story.

I have always believed that a good film doesn't just *answer* some of life's questions; it also *raises* questions. One of my goals in writing and directing *17 Miracles* was to entertain viewers while also making them think about what they are seeing. I wanted to depict in a realistic manner the hardships endured by the members of the last of the 1856 pioneer companies and do that in a way that would invite admiration for their unparalleled faith, courage, determination, and endurance. I also wanted to memorialize the divine intervention that in so many cases made survival possible. That is one of the reasons for the title of the film.

It should be noted that in some instances, I blended details of two or more stories, not to distort history but to achieve a dramatic effect. Thus *17 Miracles* is not a documentary but rather an inspiring story based on true experiences. Moreover, the film does not tell the entire story. A feature film can only scratch the surface of the events being depicted. Much more lies beneath. It is my hope that this book will fill in a few of the gaps, answer some questions, raise a few more, and invite even greater admiration for the wonderful handcart pioneers I have come to know and love. It remains for you—the viewer of the film and the reader of this book—to decide how much of a role unseen hands played in their heroic achievement.

Jolene S. Allphin: In 1999 I served as my LDS stake's historical chairman of a handcart trek planned for the summer of 2000. I began collecting individual biographical sketches of the members of the Willie, Martin, Hunt, and Hodgetts companies and their rescuers to give to the 450 participants in that reenactment. I had no idea that my calling would give rise to a book—*Tell My Story, Too*—or lead to any of the other rich experiences and friendships that have developed since that time. Not all of the stories that I have uncovered have been published, and I continue to obtain new ones. My goal is that not one of the rescuers or members of those four 1856 companies of pioneers will be forgotten and that their descendants will have a readily available place to learn about their ancestors.

In 1999 I took the list of the pioneers' names from the book *Remember,* which recounts the monumental effort undertaken by members of the Riverton Wyoming Stake to identify the members of these four groups of pioneers and their rescuers and then complete authorized temple ordinances for them. That endeavor became known as the Second Rescue. The stories of those pioneers have permeated many countries and cultures as Church members and many others have participated in handcart trek reenactments, hungered for stories of courage and faith, and learned of eternal families because of the Second Rescue.

I hoped for years that a talented filmmaker would depict some of the stories of my 1856 pioneer friends on the big screen. I was thrilled when I learned that T. C. Christensen was doing just that. Over the years, he has used his remarkable talents to bring us such films as *A Pioneer Miracle, Only a Stonecutter,* and *The John Tanner Story*—inspiring films that have brought to life the stories of early Saints whose actions demonstrated their faith, courage, and devotion to the restored gospel. So when I learned that T. C. was planning a film about the handcart pioneers, I could hardly wait to inundate him with advice, solicited or otherwise. I am grateful that he chose to use me as a historical adviser on the film and am pleased to have been a contributor to such a remarkable project.

In the wake of the popularity of *17 Miracles,* both T. C. and I have continued to be asked questions about the events it portrays. I am happy to provide here corroborating information that affirms the accuracy of those events. The spelling in quotations from pioneer records has occasionally been modernized for readability, and paragraphing sometimes altered.

Some sources, of course, are often more reliable than others—for example, a diary entry made by a participant or eyewitness at the time of an event is more reliable than an account written many years later by someone who was not present but had heard stories about the event. What you choose to accept or to discount is up to you, but you might consider this as you decide: For years I kept a folder labeled "Myths," in which I put stories that have been told for more than a century but that contain inconsistencies, inaccuracies, or specious interpretations. Yet after spending more than twelve years studying the lives of the rescuers and members of four companies of 1856 pioneers, I now view such stories quite differently, feeling that *myths* is too strong a word to describe some problematic histories.

That remarkable events were recorded by those who experienced them or were eyewitnesses to them and that those stories were then perpetuated by family traditions gives them a certain veracity and makes them worthy of study. If errors and misinterpretations of what the pioneers wrote or said have crept in, I believe in correcting such inaccuracies as they are found and verified. But we must bear in mind that if each of the nearly 2,000 individuals involved in this handcart and rescue saga should appear to us today to personally tell us his or her story, it is likely that no two accounts would be exactly the same. Ask any group of eyewitnesses to describe an automobile accident they have seen, and you will find disagreements in details. Such discrepancies are characteristic of eyewitness testimonies in any age.

In this book I attempt to provide more information about stories of true experiences depicted in *17 Miracles.* I hope you enjoyed seeing that wonderful film and will enjoy learning a little more about the people and the events it portrays.

Questions

I

Why is the film called 17 Miracles?

T. C.: The name *17 Miracles* came about because one day co-producer Ron Tanner asked me how many miracles we would portray in the film. I counted them, called him up, and said, "Seventeen. There are seventeen miracles." Something clicked, and I immediately added, "Hey! Now that's a title!" From the start, I had wanted to find a title that said much more than "This is a handcart film."

I keep a file of film ideas, and as we were finishing up

The John Tanner Story, Ron and I were talking about the ideas in that file. He really liked an idea I had in there about an incident that happened in the Martin handcart company. I decided to do some research. My first effort was buying the excellent book *The Price We Paid,* by Andrew D. Olsen. As I read it, I noticed a pattern: Over and over again, a family on the trek would be beaten down in dire circumstances and then blessed with a miracle. These were not miracles that completely solved the difficult situations but were what I call sustaining miracles. These miracles gave them some nourishment, or whatever their current need might have been, but more than that assured them that the Lord was with them.

It didn't take me long before I was hooked. I realized *that* was the story I wanted to tell—the positive side of this journey. So we were looking for a title with that connotation, and *17 Miracles* was just the ticket. We actually looked at and tested several other titles for the film, but through it all, we kept coming back to *17 Miracles.*

2

What are the 17 miracles?

T. C.: I did not want to create a film in which a miracle would happen and then DING! a bell would sound and a number would appear on the screen, signaling the viewer that a miracle had just occurred. I wanted to create discussion. The perception of miracles is a personal thing. What might be a miracle to one person might be just a coincidence to another. People have told me that they could count only five miracles in the film. Others have said they counted near thirty.

One thing has happened as I hoped it would. Many families report that after watching the film, they sit around counting, discussing, and trying to identify the miracles. I love that! That is terrific!

I decided well before the film went into production that we would never come out with a list of what the miracles are. I will provide this insight, however: If you open your mind and think in a broader way, many more than seventeen miracles will open themselves to you. It is obvious that it was a miracle that Frederick Panting looked right into the faces of his wife and children and did not recognize them, but many miracles portrayed in the film are not so obvious. I offer three examples.

First, Levi Savage. From what he learns about and then sees of the Donner Party disaster, Levi has firsthand knowledge of what can happen when a pioneer trek goes awry. After reaching the Salt Lake Valley, Levi is called on a mission to Siam and two years later "just happens" to be returning to Utah through New York. There he meets Captain James G. Willie, who asks Levi to be a subcaptain in his handcart company. So now an accomplished outdoorsman, experienced in the ways of the West, is in a leadership position with the Willie company. He was one of the first up in the morning and one of the last to bed at night. He helped the Saints through rivers, and he comforted and ministered to all. No one can say for sure how many lives Levi Savage saved, but I can say for sure it was a miracle that he just happened to be traveling through New York at that time.

Second, Elizabeth Panting. Several scenes in *17 Miracles* show a woman pulling the handcart. We may have done five or six takes of each shot, which involved the woman pulling the handcart for 20 to 30 yards each time. Emily Wadley, who plays Elizabeth Panting, told me how tiring that was to do over and over. And that was pulling a light handcart for a few yards. I think it is a miracle that a young mother such as Elizabeth Panting could actually pull a loaded handcart, mostly by herself, for almost 1,300 miles in harsh conditions and get herself and her two young children safely to Zion.

Third, Jane Panting. As we recount in the epilogue of the film, while doubting her mother's story of the cave and the dried meat, Jane Panting "just happened" to be at a Church meeting in Idaho in which she heard a talk by a man who was a survivor of the Willie handcart company. The man's telling the story of the dried meat verified and substantiated the miracle Jane's mother had described to her over the years.

Not every miracle is as obvious as a pie in the desert or two small sea biscuits that become a pan full of bread. By thinking beyond those more obvious events, I believe a viewer will be able to count twenty or more miracles.

3

Are the actors in the film members of the LDS Church? Are any of them descendants of the members of the late 1856 wagon and handcart companies or of their rescuers?

T. C.: Because *17 Miracles* was not a Church-produced film, Church membership was not a factor in who we hired. I didn't ask the actors about their Church status. I got to know all of them fairly well, however, and I can't think of a featured actor who is not a member, although there may be one or two who are not active.

Members of the Kevin and Kim Stinger family, several of whom are actors in the film, are descendants of Nathan Tanner Porter of the Hodgetts company and of rescuer John Rawlston Poole.[1] Kim Stinger plays the woman whose small child is about to be attacked by the wolves at the end of the film. That small boy (whom we also called Buffalo

Chip Boy) is played by Keaton Stinger. Kenzi Stinger plays Betsy Cunningham, who is left for dead. Kaleb Stinger plays Joseph Linford. Kalvin Stinger plays Amasa Linford. Niels Nielson is played by Kimball Stinger, and Koleman Stinger is an extra.

Many other extras were also descendants. They were amazing. They would show up day after day after day. In the winter they stood outside in freezing temperatures, dressed only in their thin pioneer wardrobe, and they happily did it all to honor their ancestors.

4

Did Elizabeth Panting's abusive husband really fail to recognize her and his own children?

T. C.: Whenever I am asked if a particular story really happened, I have to preface my remarks by saying I cannot personally vouch for it and say unequivocally that it is true. I wasn't there. All I can go on are the stories that have been passed down and the journals left behind. I can vouch for the fact that I did not make up this or any of the other miraculous events in *17 Miracles.* I wrote dialogue, illustrated personality traits, and so forth, but I did not come up with fictional characters or the miraculous incidents. The story of Elizabeth Crook Panting's abusive husband failing to recognize her and their children is fairly well known among students of Mormon history, and there are several sources for it, as Jolene describes. The scene in the film, in which a disheveled and angry Frederick Panting is seen through the rail car window standing on the platform, searching for his wife and children, is especially tense. Spousal abuse is not a recent phenomenon and was just as ugly in the 1800s as it is today. That he would actually look into the faces of his terrified wife and children and not recognize them was certainly a miracle.

Jolene: Elizabeth, born in 1828 in Gloucestershire, England, to William and Margaret Lane Crook, married Frederick Panting in 1848. They had five children together, but by the time she left England in 1856, the oldest son, Christopher (age 5), and youngest daughter, Jane (age 1) were the only surviving children.

Elizabeth, her children, and her grandchildren wrote about her experiences in traveling to Zion. According to a 2009 Daughters of Utah Pioneers history submission by S. G. Holmes, Elizabeth wrote her autobiography from entries in her own diary. It is not known where Elizabeth's diary and autobiography are now, but the correspondence of dates and places in the biographies written by Elizabeth's various descendants suggest that this diary does exist and was an original source.

B. Fay Byington collected histories written by family members about Jane Panting Bell and Jane's mother, Elizabeth, as well as other family members. This compilation, along with photographs, was sent to me by a descendant of Elizabeth. Included in this compilation is the following account from Elizabeth's son Christopher Panting:

"My father was very much against the Mormons and threatened to kill my mother if she did not stay away from the Mormons. He used to hide her shoes so she couldn't go to church. She would have to borrow her neighbor's shoes so she could go. He finally got so mean, she took her two children, Jane who was one year old and Chris who was five years old, and left him. She got on a train with her two children, but he followed her and she had to change clothes with another woman on the train so he would not recognize her."[1]

Elizabeth later married Hyrum K. Cranney. They named one of their sons Wilford Woodruff, after the apostle who had pronounced the prophecy on Elizabeth's head in England. Imagine what it meant to this boy, Wilford Woodruff Cranney, to be a living witness of the fulfillment of that blessing. He too wrote a history of his mother:

"In 1856 my mother . . . was converted to the church in England by Wilford Woodruff and was given a blessing and promise by brother Woodruff that she would reach the church headquarters in safety with her children. She was leaving her husband under his threat that he would kill her if she did so. With fear allayed by Apostle Woodruff's blessing, she went from her home to Liverpool on the train. Her husband who was hunting for her followed her into the car where she was sitting with her children. . . . However, he failed to recognize them and passed by them. He was a confirmed drunkard and mistreated her continuously.

"She boarded a sailing vessel at Liverpool in the company of emigrants and passed through many trials on the long journey to Zion. However, during the seventeen years that I lived under her influence before she died, I didn't hear her complain that she pulled a handcart . . . to Salt Lake City. . . . In 1856 she reached Salt Lake City with her little boy and girl tucked safely in the handcart even though many of their company had died on the way. . . . This was a great testimony to her from which she never wavered."[2]

5

What can you tell us about the rattlesnake scene?

T. C.: Some viewers and film critics have questioned the plausibility of the scene in which Mary Hurren and Bodil Mortensen jump over the rattlesnakes, suggesting that it seems a little farfetched. Critics have wondered if rattlesnakes really cluster, as we show them in the film. Others have asked if we used real rattlesnakes with the girls in the movie.

Through research, I learned that rattlesnakes that are disturbed sometimes migrate back to their dens. That process certainly could have been going on with the activity of the Saints moving through the area. I also read an account of contemporary individuals, not pioneers, who walked through desert terrain without paying attention to their surroundings. At some point they realized snakes were all around them. That is the kind of thing the girls may have experienced.

Jim Dix, our snake wrangler, said, "That kind of thing does happen." It is not uncommon to see many snakes out basking in the sun. In cooler weather they sometimes cluster on a rocky, warm surface.

For the filming of the scene, Jim brought out three rattlers and about ten gopher and blow snakes, which look similar to a rattler but are not poisonous. We first filmed some close-ups of the rattlers, coiled, agitated, and aggressive. Then we brought out the gopher snakes and the girls. The girls, Savannah and Bailee, actually did jump right over the top of the gopher snakes. To further create the illusion of the girls being right in the middle of the rattlers, we put a large piece of Plexiglas between Savannah and an aggressive-looking rattler. Savannah was only about four feet away from the snake, but the snake couldn't get at her.

Jolene: I love the way T. C. portrayed these innocent young girls, skipping along the trail, saying, "Make way for the Queen of England," and then whispering to each other so the snakes couldn't hear them. The account of two girls in the Willie handcart company jumping over rattlesnakes is the true story of 9-year-old Agnes Caldwell and her friend Mary Hurren, who turned eight on the trek. The girls often walked together. This first-person account comes from Agnes Caldwell:

"One day we came to a section inhabited by rattle snakes. Two of us, my friend Mary Hurren and I, would hold hands and jump. It seemed to me we were jumping for more than a mile. Due to the protecting hand of the Lord, we were not harmed."[1]

T. C. has combined characters here, with Bodil Mortensen being the friend of Mary Hurren. There is evidence from Reeder and Hurren family histories, however, that Mary was also a playmate of Bodil, as portrayed in the movie. In writing about the burial of thirteen members of the Willie handcart company at Rock Creek Hollow, Robert Reeder, Mary's uncle, recorded: "My brother-in-law James Hurren held out his 8-year-old girl Mary to see her little playmate lying among the dead."[2] Bodil Mortensen was the only young girl among those thirteen deceased persons.

This scene and others in the film illustrate the friendships that developed among children and teenagers and of the responsibilities they bore along the trail. There is, for instance, an account in the history of Agnes's brother, 14-year-old Thomas Caldwell, who suffered a broken collarbone early in the trek. This accident caused much work to fall on the shoulders of his widowed mother and his three siblings, of whom Agnes was the youngest. Thomas later wrote about how Agnes passed her time on the trail with her friends, which supports the authenticity of the film's portrayal of children at play and at work and in peril during the trek west.

In his autobiography, Thomas recalled: "Some days I could push a little on the cart but mostly I would feel so ill I could only hang on. When we would come to one of the larger streams that had to be crossed, it seemed almost too much for human nature. But as we were requested and as there was no other way, we would boldly enter the stream, helping each other the best we could. I would try my best to help my younger sisters, one at a time, through to the other side. There wasn't much I could really do as the constant pain in my collar bone was almost more than I could bear and seemed to be getting no better. Mother would treat it at night when we camped. I did however try to keep my younger sisters encouraged to keep walking. Agnes did alright as she could find friends to walk with. They would figure out some sort of a game, stories, or songs to keep their mind[s] occupied and busy."[3]

When the Willie handcart company reached the Rattlesnake Mountains near Devil's Gate, the days were still warm but nights had begun to get cold. Though Agnes Caldwell does not record exactly where her experience with rattlesnakes happened, it is conceivable that it was in this area, which is a natural habitat for the snakes, and that those snakes were migrating across the trail back to their winter habitat. The pioneer trail is very close to those mountains, definitely within a mile.

6

Was the scene intentional in which the actor portraying Levi Savage inhales a mosquito, or was that an accident during filming that was later put to good use?

T. C.: This scene, along with several others, was intended to show through humor some of the everyday events that might have taken place along the trail. I singled out Levi Savage and Ann Cooper because of the contrast between the two. Levi was a capable outdoorsman and rather rustic; Ann was more sophisticated and refined. Levi is obviously taken with her, but in his nervousness about approaching her, he makes a fool of himself on several occasions, one of them being trying to blow out of his nose a mosquito he had inhaled. We already had the best love story I could ever imagine—George Padley and Sarah Franks. I did not want the love story of Levi and Ann to interfere with or in any way trump the story of George and Sarah. So I thought humor would be a good possibility here. Those scenes were probably the easiest to write. I just thought back on all of the idiotic things I did around girls in my own dating years and wrote them in for Levi to do. If you ask me, if those antics of Levi had really happened, one of the greatest miracles would have been that Ann Cooper would actually marry him after he had been so awkward and nerdy around her through the whole trek.

Jolene: T. C. has done a masterful job in adding terrific and appropriate humor to this film. The scenes where Ann Cooper observes small incidents of Levi making a fool of himself are among my favorites.

Levi Savage himself had a great sense of humor. Consider the following diary entry from 1854 while he was on his mission in Asia. His original call was to Siam (Thailand), but he was not able to get into that country and served most of his mission in Burma (Myanmar). Levi wrote:

"Karain Vilage Monday 25 Sept 1854 This morning wen I awoke I could only finde a part of my self, for during the night the musketoes had carried a way a large portion by peas meals [piecemeal]."[1]

7

Why didn't the pioneers shoot and eat wolves or snakes?

T. C.: I was privileged to work on National Geographic's IMAX film *Lewis and Clark.* In the course of that production, I learned that the men traveling up the Missouri River in 1805 were disappointed that there was so little game left for them. It had been hunted out by Indians and trappers. And that was 51 years before the handcart companies were making their way along the Oregon Trail. We think of the 1800s West as being full of game, but the reality was that it was slim pickings. Also, I have been told that wolf meat is toxic to humans.

Jolene: A few members of the Willie company did do some hunting, but for the most part, these people were not hunters or skilled frontiersmen. Levi Savage and a few others record doing some fishing for the company. Snake meat would have probably been tasty but wouldn't have fed very many people, and they wouldn't have stopped to kill and dress them if they had seen them during the day. Wolf meat is not really edible, and the pioneers would have had to hunt the wolves at night, which would have been dangerous and caused them to miss much-needed rest. Family needs and camp duties took all their time.

Pioneer companies made provision for having meat during their journey. Often they took beef cattle to slaughter for food as it was needed along the way. Joseph Elder, for example, spent nearly four months working with George D. Grant and others to purchase and drive cattle from Kansas and Missouri to Florence, Nebraska, where the handcart companies would use some of the cattle to pull their provision wagons the final one thousand miles across the plains. Unfortunately, many of the cattle belonging to the Willie company were lost during a severe storm on the night of September 3, 1856, and were never recovered. Milk cows and beef cows were then used to pull the provision wagons, and extra weight was added to the handcarts. The branding, moving, and corralling of these animals was fraught with danger and difficulty. To eliminate the need to wrangle so many animals is one reason that Brigham Young instituted the handcart plan in the first place.

Joseph Benson Elder was a 21-year-old single man who had been attending McKendree College in Lebanon, Illinois, when he was converted to the Church. He quit school in favor of assisting the 1856 immigration. On April 25, 1856, he wrote: "This seemed to be my just duty and I accordingly determined to set about it in good faith. . . . I bade adieu to my sisters and mother and oh, how my heart did almost break to leave them, when they with tears and sobs and entreaties pled to the last for me to stay. But God had use for me in other places and I must go. So I spoke a few kind words to them and embraced them and parted not knowing when we should see each other again and I took up my line of march for the Valleys of Ephraim."[1]

On August 9, at Florence, Nebraska, Joseph wrote that the handcart companies would take part of the cattle, as expected. The Willie company arrived the next day, and Joseph recorded this description:

"The handcarts arrived true enough. There was about a hundred of them and about five hundred persons. I was agreeably surprised at the health and good feelings and cheerfulness of the camp. They traveled from 15 to 18 miles per day. The spirit of the Lord was with them. The greater portion of them was in better health than when they left Iowa City. That night a few of the Devils that walk in gents Boots who reside in Bluff city came over to fulfill their mission and do all they could against the handcart emigration. Quite a muss."[2]

Like Levi Savage, Joseph Elder wrote honest and sometimes even humorous entries in his diary regarding his experiences of working with cattle:

"Wednesday 16th [July 1856] We had an awful day's work today of branding cattle. They tried often to kill us but we eluded their efforts. There was about forty we could not brand any way or how."[3]

"Friday 18th Today we crossed the Missouri River. We

swam sum, feryed sum, and drounded sum. They fought us like tigers, etc."[4]

"Monday 5th [August] Traveled hard. The meanest cattle to drive that I ever had anything to do with. Sold one of our cows that tried to kill us so often for $25.00."[5]

Another provision pioneer companies made was to assign men to hunt for the camp. One of the most common animals they hunted on the plains was buffalo. Several entries in Levi Savage's diary describe times when he went hunting to obtain meat for the company. Most often he records hunting with Joseph Elder, who had become a trusted assistant to Captain Willie. These two excerpts from Levi's diary give some insight:

"Buffalo Creek Monday 1st Sept 1856.

"Today we traveled about 18 miles. This evening we killed a buffalo, & a cow, for beef; the cow was shot 11 times before she fell. I never saw a beast so murdered before."[6]

"Chutah Lakes, Wednesday 3rd Sept 1856.

"At 12 o'clock, the Brethren killed two buffalo near the road. We took the meat on hand carts. Traveled 16 miles, & encamped without wood. Cooked our food with buffalo chips. Bro J. Elder and I went on horseback and endeavored to get a buffalo calf or cow. The old bulls would not let us have any. They formed themselves in a battle array, ready to receive their enemy. There were large herds to be seen in all directions. We did not get to camp until after dark."[7]

Joseph Elder also tells of some buffalo hunting incidents: "We now began to see buffalo off from the road. I got impatient at a distant view of them so I went out for a hunt. I chased a herd 4 or 5 miles, shot at them, but to no affect. I had to return to camp with only a prairie dog.

"The buffalo is an awkward looking animal, especially when they run. Their motions much resemble the elephant."[8]

"[John A.] Jost and I continued the hunt. We at last found 2 old bulls. We fired upon them but our eyes had deceived us. We was too far off. After several shots we succeeded in killing one. With wonder and great delight we examined him for it was an enormous big old Bull. I sat down upon him to keep the wolves off whilst Brother Jost went to camp. I had a pretty lonesome time for it was dark out. At last he came with lots of men and carts to cut him up and haul it to camp. We had a jolly time. The first buffalo in camp. When I got to camp I was tired and hungry so I and Brother Jost cut off some of the hump, a great big chunk and roasted it. I thought I never tasted so good meat in all my life. It is very healthy meat and we had a real feast etc.

"We next went over the hills which are in the Platte bottom. They are wholly surrounded by a level plain. Just as we got through or rather on the top, a large herd of buffalo started from below the road and ran directly across towards the north just as the carts were passing. They ran helter skelter right through the company. The company was pretty hungry for meat and to see the buffalo come right to them seemed to them as a great blessing of kind Providence. The scene that followed would have made a hunter laugh to see them shoot. Some with shot, others with little fizees that would hardly have upset a june bug come tearing along and up and pop pop they would go. But some of them had muskets and amongst the whole they managed to kill two. I was too far behind to help any, being with the wagons but I could see the performance and then of all the bragging about who killed them. Some declared they hit him after he fell etc.

"Well, my time was mostly employed in furnishing the camp in meat, most of which was buffalo. Many were the interesting hunts which I had, for hunting buffalo is the greatest sport for me of any sport that I ever participated in. . . . after we got onto the Sweet Water River I mostly gave up hunting for game got scarce."[9]

8

Was Levi Savage's reluctance to begin the trek so late in the season accurately portrayed?

T. C.: This is one of the few dialogue scenes in the film for which I did not write any dialogue. I didn't have to. I only had to edit what was recorded by those who were present.

The words that Levi Savage and Captain Willie say in this scene come right out of eyewitnesses' journals.

Jolene: On August 13, the Willie handcart company was gathered together near Florence, Nebraska, to discuss their journey and give the people an opportunity to decide if they wanted to continue. This would be their last chance to back out, as they were pretty much leaving civilization at that point. Close to 100 people did drop out of the Willie company and did not continue to the Salt Lake Valley that year.

The weight of responsibility on the shoulders of the captains of this company was enormous. It was at this meeting that Levi Savage voiced his honest opposition to continuing.

Emma James, then 18, wrote of this meeting: "Brother [Levi] Savage, with tears streaming down his cheeks he pleaded with the people. 'Brothers and sisters, wait until spring to make this journey. Some of the strong may get through in case of bad weather, but the bones of the weak and old will strew the way.'"[1]

George Cunningham, age 15 at the time, wrote of Levi's heartfelt plea: "Some stayed [in Florence], and would not go any farther. In fact, we were told that if any wanted to stop that they might do so, but the counsel was to go on to the valleys. I can remember of being at a meeting one night when Brother Levi Savage, a returning missionary, arose and spoke. He counseled the old, weak, and sickly to stop until another spring. The tears commenced to flow down his cheeks and he prophesied that if such undertook the journey at that late season of the year, that their bones would strew the way."[2]

Joseph Elder was not planning on traveling with the Willie company across the plains and wrote in his diary only a very brief account of the meeting that night: "Tuesday 13th Meeting at night. Sweet singing—a favorite song composed by E. Hill."[3]

Interestingly, the song Joseph Elder referred to is our present-day hymn "As Sisters in Zion," and the "E. Hill" was 20-year-old Emily Hill, who traveled with her 23-year-old sister, Julia Hill, in the Willie handcart company. Some time before Emily left England, having been ostracized by her family because of her conversion to Mormonism, Elder John Halliday blessed her and prophesied that "she should write in prose and in verse and thereby comfort the hearts of thousands."[4] Originally ten verses long, Emily's poem was, more than 100 years later, set to a tune written by Janice Kapp Perry and included in the present LDS hymnbook.[5]

Two days later, leaders of the Willie company decided they needed Joseph Elder to continue with them. He had previously planned to travel with the last of the returning missionaries and immigration agents. Joseph recorded: "Thurs. 15th . . . At night about 10 o'clock I was waked up by sum of the Boys. They said I was wanted. I got up and went down to the corral. They proposed my starting with the present handcart company on the morrow and drive their team until they overtook us on the plains. Short notice. However, I determined to start for Utah."[6]

Levi Savage, who had been recruited in a similar manner, wrote about another meeting held just before this request was made of Joseph Elder: "Florence Nebraska Territory. Friday 15th August 1856. Today we continued preparations for starting. I wrote a letter to my Brother Alanson, &c [etcetera]. Evening we held meeting. Elders McGaw; Kimble; Grant; Vancott addressed the Saints; exhorted them to go forward regardless of the consequences."[7]

We can almost hear between the lines of these short phrases the underlying stress and tension. T. C. has captured that tension very well in *17 Miracles.*

The first two groups of one hundred each started out the next day and moved just five miles. Levi and his hundred were with them. To give some sense of what they were facing, consider what Levi recorded the next day: "Little Papaw, Nebraska, Sunday 17th Aug 1856. This morning I wrote a letter to my brother Alanson in Illinois and one to Joseph Bouton, Conn[ecticut]. I then went back to town with six men and got thirty-seven beeves & milch Cows.

Our wagons are loaded with 35 or 40 Hundred of provisions and we yet want 25 Hundred or more and have no wagon, nor can't purchase one to haul it in."[8]

9

Who was the mysterious man who gave Elizabeth Panting the dried meat?

T. C.: Several pioneers told about being helped by someone they did not know, but none of the pioneer accounts describe the helper's physical appearance. For all I know, these helpers could have been the same person. In any case, I decided to combine them into one character, depicted in the film as the mysterious stranger who leads Elizabeth Panting to a cache of dried meat. When she asks him who he is, his response is simply, "Like you, I am a traveler" (a line I wrote). I used his appearances to create a thread of continuity. If you watch the film closely, you'll see him on other occasions. He represents the persons various Saints mentioned, but more than that, in the film his character is a way of saying the Lord was watching over them. I have been asked many times who I think the person was. I don't know, and I don't try to say. I just portrayed what the pioneers said happened.

Jolene: The pioneers and their descendants spoke about these mysterious helpers. First, Elizabeth Panting. After her arrival in Utah, Elizabeth married William Wilkes, with whom she had two children before separating from him. She married Hyrum K. Cranney in 1864 and gave birth to seven more children. Elizabeth died in 1891 and was buried in the city cemetery in Logan, Utah.

I have interviewed Elizabeth's granddaughter June Cranney Monson twice in her home. Although June, who is the daughter of Elizabeth's son Frank P. Cranney, did not know her grandmother personally, she knew her aunt Jane Panting Bell very well. She told me that Jane often visited their family in Star Valley, Wyoming, and loved to tell stories from her mother's life. The following are excerpts from one of June Monson's written accounts:

"I can't remember when I first knew my Aunt Jane Bell, or when I first heard the story of Grandmother Cranney and her trek across the plains. As a child I remember being aware that Grandmother had been with the Willies handcart company and that she had suffered a great deal on the way to Salt Lake City.

"I remember hearing about Aunt Jane being so sick [lying in the handcart] and how Grandmother didn't dare stop to take care of her and she would just go on and call [back] to her small son, Chris, and ask him if Jane was dead yet.

I used to think about this and wonder how she could have stood it.

"When I was about fifteen, Aunt Jane came up to the ranch in Star Valley to visit us. She was such a little, quick, spunky character that I loved her very dearly. . . . While she was visiting us she told me the story of her Mother's experience on the plains. . . . Grandmother Cranney and the other members of the Willies handcart company were in terrible shape. The supplies had dwindled until nearly all of the people were starving. Grandmother was out gathering some buffalo chips to make a small fire to warm what little food that they had left for her children. She had on a long, full apron and had almost filled it with the buffalo chips. A man came up to her and talked to her and asked how the members of the company were. She told him that most of them were starving and he asked her to follow him and maybe he could help a little. Aunt Jane said that her mother shook out her apron and went with him. They went over a small hill and were out of sight of the camp. In the side of the hill was sort of a cave and he led Grandmother into the cave. On one side of the cave was a lot of dried buffalo meat hanging up.

"The man loaded as much meat in Grandmother's apron as she could carry and told her to share with the other people. Then he led her out of the cave and to the top of a small hill and pointed out the camp below and told her not to get lost. As Grandmother turned back to him to thank him after she had looked where he had pointed to the camp, he had disappeared. She looked for the cave and could find no trace of it, but she still had the dried meat. She went back to camp and divided the meat out to the ones that were in the most need and it saved many lives.

"Years later when Aunt Jane was an elderly woman, she was in Pocatello, Idaho, visiting her daughter. It was on Mother's Day and her daughter took her to church with her. I remember Aunt Jane said that she hesitated about going because she didn't want to take some other Mother's gift, since she didn't belong to that ward. . . . During this same program an elderly man got up to talk and he told of coming to Utah with his family when he was a small boy with the Willies handcart company and how they were starving and some sister in the company had received some dried meat in some miraculous way and had shared it and he was very grateful to that sweet sister.

"Aunt Jane said she cried when she heard this because so many people had made fun of her story of her mother's experience until she had almost come to doubt it herself. She talked to the gentleman and told him that she was a baby with that company and that it was her mother who had received the meat. She said that it was wonderful to have another witness of this wonderful experience."[1]

Another descendant wrote of Elizabeth's miraculous

experience this way: "It was during this trip to Zion on 14 October when another reduction was made in rations that my great-grandmother, Elizabeth Crook Panting, was out gathering buffalo chips for a fire. Suddenly and seemingly from out of nowhere a man came to her and asked if the company were in need. She told him how they were starving and how great [was] their need. The man told her to follow him. So dumping her apron of buffalo chips, she followed. He led her to a cave and took her in. A lot of dried meat was hanging in the cave. The man filled my great-grandmother's apron with meat and told her to take it to the company. She turned to go, then remembering she hadn't thanked him, she turned to do so, but the man was gone, also gone was the cave. My great-grandmother took the meat to Captain Willie and told him of her experiences. Captain Willie said it must have been one of the Three Nephites."[2]

10

Are there other accounts of the ministration of angels?

Jolene: As T. C. noted, several accounts record someone appearing to help them. For example, Patience Loader, a member of the Martin company, wrote:

"I will say we traveled on all day in the snow, but the weather was fine and in the middle of the day the sun was quite warm. Sometime in the afternoon a strange man appeared to me as we were resting. As we got up the hill he came and looked in my face. He says, 'Is you Patience?' I said, 'Yes.' He said again, 'I thought it was you. Travel on. There is help for you. You will come to a good place. There is plenty.' With this he was gone. He disappeared. I looked but never saw where he went. This seemed very strange to me. I took this as someone sent to encourage us and give us strength."[1]

After the Martin company's last crossing of the Platte on October 19, Aaron Jackson (age 31) died. His widow, Elizabeth Horrocks Jackson, wrote: "It will be readily perceived that under such circumstances I had become despondent. I was six or seven thousand miles from my native land, in a wild, rocky, mountain country, in a destitute condition, the ground covered with snow, the waters covered with ice, and I with three fatherless children with scarcely [anything] to protect them from the merciless storms. When I retired to bed that night, being the 27th of Oct., I had a stunning revelation. In my dream, my husband stood by me and said, 'Cheer up, Elizabeth, deliverance is at hand.'"[2]

Grace Wignall, whose husband, William, was captain of the first hundred of the Martin company, told about a heavenly manifestation:

"We crossed the Platte River for the last time. That evening the snow fell about 18 inches deep. . . . the camp moved about nine miles to a bluff called the Red Point. We were there about nine days. The snow was then about two feet deep. We had only one-fourth [pound] of flour per day. My husband was taken sick and I called in the Elders to administer to him. He recovered immediately. I then went to bed and a Heavenly Messenger came to my bed-side and said, 'Cheer up, Sister Wignall, there are mules, horses, and wagon teams coming to meet you with provisions and clothing from the Valley. Tomorrow morning, when Mary Ann Riley is combing your hair, there will be a man with two pack mules come into camp.' Sure enough, just as she was combing my hair about 9 A.M. Joseph [A.] Young and a brother, who now lives in Provo but the name I have forgotten, came into camp just as I had seen them."[3]

Elizabeth Jackson and Grace Wignall each recorded the visit of a messenger on October 27. The express rescue party of Joseph A. Young, Abel Garr, and Daniel W. Jones found the stranded Martin company at the Bessemer Bend of the Platte River at the area known as Red Buttes on October 28. It seems that these angelic messages would qualify as what T. C. calls sustaining miracles. They were received at a time when the Martin company had pretty much lost all hope of survival.

As many as 56 members of the Martin company died during the 12 days preceding the arrival of the rescuers at the camp.

By October 16, the weather had started to get much colder. Feed for the already weakened cattle was scarce this late in the season, and the flour rations for the Martin company were reduced. The next day, October 17, the Martin company reduced their baggage from the previous allotment of 17 pounds per person to 10 pounds for adults and 5 pounds for children. The situation was so desperate that "good blankets and other bedding and clothing were burned as they could not be carried further, though needed more badly than ever, for there was yet 400 miles of winter to go through."[4]

On October 19, the Martin company crossed the North Platte River for the last time at the Upper Crossing. The Church had operated a ferry at that site a few years before, but it was no longer in use. The Martin company had passed a toll bridge about five miles before they reached Upper Crossing, but the toll was too high for company members to pay. Known as Richard's Bridge or Platte Bridge, it was near a trading post sometimes known as Fort Bridge.

As the Martin company crossed the wide and swift Platte River, the first winter storm descended. Sharp ice cakes already floating down the river cut the pioneers' legs. Wind and snow added to their misery. Some individuals were swept off their feet and carried downstream. Many were the heroics of that day as members of the Hodgetts and Hunt wagon companies and the Martin handcart company helped to carry others across the river. George Padley was one of the rescuers from within the ranks of the Martin company. The exposure he suffered during this service contributed to his death some two weeks later. The storm and the icy river crossing caused much suffering for the people and their animals. They made little progress over the next few days.

On October 20, they moved only three and a half miles through deep snow and suffered a further reduction in rations. The next day snow fell again, and the Martin company was unable to move at all. At this same time, the advance rescue team led by George D. Grant arrived at the similarly stranded Willie camp, about 100 miles farther west than the Martin company. Ten of the 14 relief wagons were sent on for the rescue of the Martin, Hunt, and Hodgetts companies.

The Martin company was again unable to move on October 22, and the following day they traveled only 5 or 6 miles to the Red Buttes area at Bessemer Bend on the Platte River. That day Willie company members crossed Rocky Ridge in a blizzard.

On October 24, the Martin company was unable to move. The Willie company, by then at Rock Creek, was also unable to move. Fifteen members of the Willie company were buried there, including Bodil Mortensen and young

Niels Nielson. In the movie, little Niels is shown with the elephant that Levi Savage had carved for him in his hands. The relationship depicted in *17 Miracles* between Levi and Niels is good storytelling and in several scenes leads the viewer to imagine what Levi was feeling as he thinks of his own little boy.

The Martin company was unable to move for the next three days and suffered a further reduction in rations. Captain Edward Martin called his people together to determine what to do at this critical time. Some of the company members told of the events:

Louisa Mellor. "At last the Company gave up and decided they could go no further. We all gathered around and held a meeting, praying God to help us, as we knew it was Him alone who could deliver us from death. We were happy and willing to die for a just cause."[5]

Peter McBride. "A meeting was held. It was decided that we could go no further, the snow so deep and no food. We were doomed to starvation. They gave me a bone of an ox that had died. I cut off the skin and put the bone in the fire to roast. And when it was done some big boys came and ran away with it. Then I took the skin and boiled it, drank the soup, and ate the skin, and it was a good supper. The next day we had nothing to eat but some bark from trees."[6]

Elizabeth Sermon. "We traveled on until a heavy

snowstorm overtook us and further progress could not be made. . . . The Captain called us all together and stated that we must lay our bodies down, and 'were we willing to do so for the Gospel's sake?'"[7]

Eliza Morton. "Worn out with the wearisome journey, half-starved, footsore, and heartsick, Eliza Morton often sat on a bank when a stop was made along the dreary journey, surrounded by deep and glistening snow, and thought of the home she had forsaken. Eliza also related in later years how when the weather was below zero and she carried water from a river to camp, the handles of the buckets would freeze to her hands. So desperate was their situation that when they were almost without food and snowbound at Red Buttes, their captain, Edward Martin, stood before them as they sat huddled about the embers of a dying campfire and asked whether if it should be the will of the Lord that they perish there, they were willing to submit to his will. Each man and woman raised his or her hand as a signal of submission. Characteristic of her faith, Eliza Morton remarked: 'I held up my hand, but I didn't believe we were going to die.'"[8]

It is hard to imagine what it would mean to these people who had traveled hundreds of miles, experienced encouraging miracles along the way, to come to this. After the meeting, 19-year-old Jane Bitton was resigned to the probability that this was the end. She said that if she was going to die, she would die clean. She took clean underclothing and went to the nearby river and washed herself in its icy water. As she was dressing, she heard a great commotion and shouting from the camp. She hurriedly finished dressing and started back when she met an elderly Scotsman who was crying. (This was probably 67-year-old George P. Waugh, counselor to Edward Martin and leader of the invalids.) She asked him what was wrong. He answered, "Aye, lassie, we're saved! We're saved!" Jane replied, "Then what in the world are you cryin' for?"[9]

It was October 28, and help had finally come, just as the angelic visitors had promised Sister Wignall and Sister Jackson. These were mortal angels, with messages of hope that the rescue wagons were coming. The three express riders were Joseph Angell Young, Daniel Webster Jones, and Abel Garr. Albert Jones, then 16 years old, described his impression of the arrival of Joseph A. Young:

"At Red Butte our position was critical. After laying over here some few days, the snow on the ground and very cold, we were rescued by the gallant and brave Joseph A. Young, the son of President Brigham Young . . . as he came down the declivity onto the bottom where our camp was located on the light colored mule, which was entirely lost sight of, for all that appeared was a man with blue wings flying to our rescue—the illusion being produced by Brother Joseph A. Young wearing an old blue Government Overcoat

Dragoon style with the old US Button . . . enormously large in skirts and Cape—the joy of the camp and the immediate effect his arrival had cannot be described, men and women fell on their knees, some cried, some laughed—some prostrated themselves on the earth, others prayed aloud, giving thanks to God for deliverance. Joseph A. was well known to the Saints for he had trod the deck of the good ship *Horizon* and helped at the embarkation of the greater number of those men and women there present and numbers more who were laid at rest in their lonely graves by the way side. [Joseph A. had returned from his mission to England this very season of 1856.] He was immediately besieged by the camp, who surrounded him asking questions thick and fast of news of coming aid from the Valleys—he immediately announced help at hand—flour at Willow Springs—and ordered the issuance of full rations of flour that night. Now joy took hold of the camp and prayers of thanksgiving ascended from our hearts and the evening hymns at prayer time were sung with some degree of the animation that characterized the services at the earlier period of our journey."[10]

In an account given for a newspaper article later in his life, Albert Jones referred to Joseph A. Young's arrival as that of a "big blue-winged angel."[11]

II

What about angels who were not seen?

Jolene: *17 Miracles* portrays two accounts of angels who were not seen. Consider Louisa Mellor's own words about the pie delivered miraculously for her mother, Mary Ann Payne Mellor:

"My mother, being still weak, finally gave up and said she could go no further. The company could not wait for her, so she bade my father goodbye and kissed each one of the children Godspeed. Then my mother sat down on a boulder and wept. I told my sister Elizabeth to take good care of the twins and the rest of the family, and that I would stay with Mother. I went a few yards away and prayed with faith that God would help us, that He would protect us from devouring wolves, and asked that He would let us reach camp. As I was going back to where my mother was sitting, I found a pie in the road. I picked it up and gave it to my mother to eat, and after resting awhile we started on our journey, thanking God for the blessings. A few miles before we reached camp we met my father coming out to meet us. What a joyful meeting that was! We arrived in camp at 10:00 P.M. o'clock. Many times after that Mother felt like giving up and quitting; but then would remember how wonderful the Lord had been to spare her so many times, and offered a prayer of gratitude instead. So she went on her way rejoicing while walking the blood-stained path of snow."[1]

Perhaps a pie was missing from someone's kitchen in Utah that day. Or maybe pies are baked in the spirit world. That will be a question to ask when I get there. When one of my daughters watched the movie with me, she asked me if the pie was warm. I don't know, of course, but one Mellor descendant told me that family tradition says it was a meat pie.

This heavenly delivery of sustaining food was not the first miracle for 36-year-old Mary Ann Payne Mellor in helping her get to Zion in 1856. It was miraculous that Sister Mellor had survived to board the ship at Liverpool. Extremely ill from the birth of conjoined twins, who died soon afterward, Mary Ann had sent most of her family onto the ship, determined to join them in Zion later. The ship had actually left the harbor, but after being delayed by storms and a mutiny of the sailors on board, it returned to port. During that time Mary Ann mustered enough strength to change her mind. She was carried on a stretcher from her sickbed to the shore and was helped to board the ship. A blessing by Elders Cyrus Wheelock and George Goddard told her that her mission on earth was not yet finished. They promised Mary Ann that she would live to reach Utah and "see her seed in Zion."[2]

In 1881, Louisa Mellor wrote more of the family's story, affirming the promises made to her mother. The following passage provides a firsthand description of the hardships endured by the Saints, even before the trek itself, let alone afterwards on the wintry plains of Wyoming:

"Finally we were called to immigrate to Utah and leave our relatives and friends, which was quite a trial. The hardest was to leave my poor grandfather. I think I can see him now, although he is sleeping in his grave—I hope in peace, for he was a good man. He wept and offered money to his dear daughter, my dear mother, but relief was offered too late, for this gospel was more [to them] than anything else. My dear mother grieved for her dear old father, which brought sickness on, and she came near losing her life.

"When my parents left England they had seven small children, as Salina Ann, and Mary Ann, had died when very young. The twins, Emma and Clara, were the youngest, and two-and-one-half years old at that time. We stayed a while at Liverpool to secure our passage, and while there, Mother gave birth to another pair of twins, who died shortly after birth. They were Siamese twins and just like little dolls. The doctor said he buried them in the ocean, but later we found that he had preserved them and had made a fortune with them. Mother was so ill the doctor gave her up and said she could not live, that if we took her on board the ship the sharks would follow until she died.

Brother Wheelock and Brother Goddard and others administered to her and promised her that she would live and come to Utah, that she would see her seed in Zion, and that her mission on this earth was not yet finished.

"While we were in Liverpool I spent my 16th birthday. It was on May 23, 1856, and a sad one it was for me, as I was left alone with a sick mother and a little sister two and one-half years old, as my father had to take the rest of the family and go aboard. The ship sailed out to sea so I thought my father could not come back again, but he did." Delayed by storms and a mutiny of sailors on board, the ship returned to port, where Louisa's father found those who had stayed behind. "My mother was very low, but Father said if she wanted to go he wouldn't give her up, so they got a stretcher and carried her in a bed to the sea shore and then in a steamboat out to sea to catch the vessel where the rest of the children were. When we got to the vessel the Captain asked, 'What are you bringing a dead woman here for, and why don't you throw her in the sea?' But they got her on board and some of the sisters tended her. I had the care of the family of nine—seven children. We were five and one-half weeks on board and I used to go and see my dear mother twice a day, and take care of the children. Mother was able to gain a little strength, but not able to do anything, so I had nearly the entire care of the family.

"We left Liverpool under the leadership of Edward

Martin, on the ship *Horizon.* There were 856 Saints in all who were coming to North America. Storms arose and the ship tipped to and fro and delayed us from a straight voyage; however, on the evening of 28 June 1856 the ship cast anchor in the Boston Harbor. By this time my mother was getting better and able to get around some, so we joined the Saints and went west to Iowa.

"After landing we all took what might be called cattle cars, which was thought good enough for the Mormons, until we reached Iowa. We remained in Iowa City from July 8 to July 28, 1856, where my father secured work, and with the means was able to get two handcarts and some food and clothes to make the journey across the plains.

"[We left] Florence, with 575 souls, 148 handcarts, and 7 wagons. It was a pretty sight to see those 575 saints out with handcarts, singing handcart songs: 'Some may push and some may pull as we go marching up the hill, a-merrily on our way we go until we reach the valley, and long before the valley's reached we will meet with music sweet and friends so dear, which supply our hearts with cheer.' . . . We were the last handcart company to leave for the Salt Lake Valley that year.

"One thing happened that convinced me that if we put our trust in our Heavenly Father he will answer our prayers when we are in need. While we were in Iowa we had to burn or sell our things because we could not haul them, and so as we were two miles from the city, Mother and I went [back] to town to sell a few things in the shape of clothes. We walked from house to house before we could sell them, and as we were so long, when we got back to camp they had had dinner and started again, and the captain came back and met us. My poor mother was sick after that, but the Lord protected us from wild beasts and gave us food to eat.

"Mother was put in the wagon for a while. We traveled twenty miles a day. Then my father took sick. He got so weak he could not pull his handcart, so I had to help him. We had two handcarts; my sister and I pulled one, and father and the younger sister pulled the other one. But father got weaker so we had to lighten our load again, and as 17 pounds were all that was allowed for each adult we had but little to spare, but a box of books and records which Father valued very much. But what could we do but let them go? So as we were going through [a town in Iowa] we stopped and I helped carry them in a house and we got the privilege to leave them till we sent for them, but we never got them again.

"While crossing the plains, trials of different kinds were our portion. Many fainted and fell by the wayside. Many a mound was dug and a fervent prayer uttered for those gone and those left, that God would spare them to reach Zion. We were so fatigued and hungry that we would stop and get rawhide to chew on, as our food was diminished. We tried to keep a little flour as long as we could, to make porridge for the children; at first it was biscuits; then pancakes; then porridge. Often we would cook a hide or piece of it to get a little strength; it being winter, we could not find weeds to help out.

"The first snow storm left about two feet of snow on the ground and we began to feel very nervous. We had to wade through more streams, and sometimes up to our waists, and when we got through our clothes would freeze on us until we reached camp and made a fire to thaw out. And so we traveled on until a great many gave up and a great many died, mostly old people. At last the snow got to be four and five feet deep and often we had to shovel a road before we could move. Thus our traveling was very slow and our provisions nearly gave out.

"The outlook was very discouraging. The captain called a meeting and told us there was only enough food for one more day and asked us if we would rather have it all or divide it into three days. We all agreed to divide it. And despite our desperate situation we sang the handcart songs. One was, 'If we should die before our journey's through, Happy day! All is well!' The camp gave up to die, if need be, and scarcely a dry eye was left to see the dying."[3]

After the Mellor family and other emigrants had sailed from Liverpool, Elders Wheelock and Goddard left

England with President Franklin D. Richards and other returning missionaries. They were among those portrayed in *17 Miracles* as passing the handcart companies on the plains. Once they reached the Valley, Elders Wheelock and Goddard turned around and traveled hundreds of miles back on the trail to find and rescue the belated companies. At the time the rescuers left Salt Lake City, journals recorded the weather in what is now Wyoming as "splendid" and even "hot,"[4] but the travelers were in dire circumstances by the time rescuers reached them. Cyrus Wheelock served as the chaplain of the first rescue party to reach the Mellor family. Louisa Mellor wrote:

"Brother Wheelock and Brother Goddard . . . asked for James Mellor. When they saw him they were stunned! A man of 38 years of age with hair as white as the driven snow! Indeed, the trials and tribulations, the hardships and the deprivations they had suffered from England to Salt Lake Valley had taken its toll. They took him in their arms and wept! They also greeted my mother, to whom they had promised life and that she would live to see Zion."[5]

Louisa's father, James Mellor, was the first member of the Mellor family to join the Church, in 1844. He served as a missionary, and one of his first converts was his mother-in-law, Charlotte Squires Payne. Too ill at the time to be baptized or to consider emigration, Charlotte "begged James to go to Zion and there attend to her salvation."[6] She died soon after making that request. The Mellor family performed the temple ordinance work after reaching their Rocky Mountain Zion.

Louisa concluded her autobiographical sketch with a heartfelt plea to her descendants that echoes that of her grandmother:

"Now, my children and grandchildren, or who are living today, the year of Jubilee [1880], we, your parents, to those who are faithful, wish you, as we shall be in the graves, to hunt up our records, and if possible do some more of our work as we have not had time to do all. And also for any of our posterity that have died and not finished their work, and if it is consistent with the will of our Father in Heaven, we your parents, will aid you and bless you in all righteousness."[7]

Another account of unseen angels comes from Francis Webster of the Martin company, but it is combined with the character of Levi Savage for the purposes of *17 Miracles:*

"I have pulled my handcart when I was so weak and weary from illness and lack of food that I could hardly put one foot ahead of the other. I have looked ahead and seen a patch of sand or a hill slope and I have said, I can go only that far and there I must give up for I cannot pull the load through it. I have gone to that sand and when I reached it, the cart began pushing me! I have looked back many times to see who was pushing my cart, but my eyes saw no one. I knew then that the angels of God were there.

"Was I sorry that I chose to come by handcart? No!

Neither then nor any minute of my life since. The price we paid to become acquainted with God was a privilege to pay and I am thankful that I was privileged to come in the Martin handcart company."[8]

These words are even more meaningful when we learn that they were spoken by Francis Webster when he was an old man who had lived a life of service to God and his community. In 2008 a statue of Francis Webster was placed on Main Street in the historic district of Cedar City, Utah, where he served as mayor from 1872 to 1876. His memory is still revered by many. In 1856 he was a wealthy 25-year-old newlywed when he left England, but he gave all his wealth to the Emigration Fund except what he needed for his own handcart and provisions. His wife, Ann Elizabeth Parsons Webster, was not one whit behind him in faithfulness. Their first baby, Amy, was born on the plains on September 27, 1856, a mere three weeks before the first winter storms descended.

The Websters were in the Valley for only two days before they continued their journey another 300 miles to southern Utah at the request of Brigham Young. Francis was so grateful for his blessings that he did something remarkable. He recorded in his journal: "I paid my Tithing on the little clothing I brought with me. . . . My own feet were badly frozen on the journey."[9]

Amy Webster wrote about the determination of her mother, Ann Elizabeth Webster:

"A few days after they reached Cedar [City], representatives of the Benevolent Society called to see if they could not help them, but mother's independence prompted her to say, 'No' unless they had some soap they would lend her. They sent the soap and mother paid them back, the first time that she made soap. It was not charity, but work that she wanted."[10]

Ann Elizabeth Webster too was so grateful and faithful that she consecrated the rest of her life to serving and giving charity to others.

12

Did George Padley actually write the poem to Sarah Franks?

T. C.: In Jolene's book, *Tell My Story, Too,* I came across a poem that John Jaques had written to his wife Zilpah.[1] It gave me the idea to have George write Sarah a poem along the way, which Sarah then discovers at his death. I used the first stanza of Jaques's poem, modified the second stanza, and then wrote the rest of it myself. It was my first writing of a poem for a movie, and I really loved the experience.

This is an example of something that is not factual in

the film but is true to the spirit of these great pioneers. So little is known of these kinds of details, but it is entirely possible that George wrote his sweetheart some poetry during the evening hours around the fires.

13

Were Sarah Franks and George Padley really engaged? Did Sarah eventually marry?

T. C.: A year after arriving in the Salt Lake Valley, Sarah Ann Franks became the third wife of Thomas Sloan Mackay. Thomas died when Sarah's youngest child was only six years old. I've been told that when President Faust asked whether the sealing of Sarah Franks and George Padley had been performed, he was told that Sarah had been sealed to another man during her lifetime. Apparently President Faust replied by saying something like, "Sarah and George earned it. We'll let the Lord sort it out."

Jolene: The story of how Sarah's engagement and the identity of her fiancé became known is a fascinating one. Family tradition held that Sarah, a member of the Martin company, was engaged to a young man, and they were planning to be married once they reached the Salt Lake Valley. The identity of the young man was not certain, but the family believed he had died at Martin's Cove. When the Second Rescue project became known, Kathleen Thacker of Salt Lake City telephoned President Kim McKinnon, of the Riverton Wyoming Stake presidency, to ask for help in identifying Sarah's fiancé and later to tell him she had learned Sarah's fiancé was named George Padley.[1] That information was soon confirmed when, "as a result of a *Church News* article, a journal was sent to President Lorimer from Johannesburg, South Africa. In the journal there was one entry that read: 'Sarah Ann Franks is betrothed to George Padley.' . . .

"It was later learned that George Padley had overexerted himself in trying to help other members of the handcart company. He had gotten wet and chilled from the winter wind. He slipped into hypothermia and died. Sarah Franks was so in love with George Padley that she did not want wolves to ravage his lifeless body. She therefore took off her shawl, probably the only thing she had to stay warm, and had the brethren wrap his body in it and suspend him in a tree. The last thing Sarah saw as she left the Cove was George's body hanging in the tree in her shawl.

"During President James E. Faust's visit to Martin's Cove, President McKinnon recited the Sarah Franks and George Padley story as the group stood looking off into the Cove from the top of the sand dune. President Faust was very moved by the story. With a tear in his eye he said it had to be one of the great love stories of the western migration."[2]

My information regarding the death of George Padley at Martin's Cove comes from the biography of Jesse Soar Taylor, who was 10 years old in 1856. He was traveling with his 12-year-old brother, William, and his 31-year-old widowed mother, Mary Soar Taylor. Jesse later remembered "seeing 15 of his fellow travelers buried in one grave in Martin's Hollow. One young man named George Padley came to his mother and said, 'Mary, I feel so weak, will you make me a little gruel?' She said, 'Yes.' Her feet were frozen so badly the captain insisted on young Padley getting his own fuel to make enough fire to prepare the meal. He did so, drank it [the gruel], retired, and died during the night."[3]

Years later, on February 20, 1881, Mary wrote to her grandson John C. Taylor a letter that was placed in a Relief Society chest to be opened fifty years later. Her testimony is poignant:

"Many had their limbs badly frozen, myself and William among the number. . . . I could not stand on my feet for three months after I arrived. . . . for the benefit of my grandchildren and others . . . I also add my testimony of the divinity of this work. I know it is the work of God and I hope and trust that any of my posterity that may come in possession of this may be strengthened in their faith by it and be worthy of such parentage for truly we suffered much for the truth's sake but the reward of the faithful is sure."[4]

14

What more can you tell us about George Padley's body being wrapped in his sweetheart's shawl and placed in a tree?

T. C.: The scene of George's death is one I took something of a liberty with. It would have been improper for George and Sarah to be alone at night under the handcart, as I portrayed them for George's death. But it was too unsatisfying to see them separated at this pinnacle moment, so I put them together. George's "burial," however, was not something I invented.

Jolene: Some historians have questioned the idea of this tree "burial" of George Padley. It is unknown if Sarah Franks kept a diary or ever wrote of this event herself, but several family histories verify this story. An account in *Descendants of Thomas Mackay—Utah Pioneer* includes information about the tree burial in the shawl and indicates that Sarah and her unnamed sweetheart had planned to be married when they reached Zion.[1]

A biography written by one of Sarah's descendants who knew her personally states that Sarah and "her sweetheart were known as the sweethearts of their company. They talked much and planned of their home in the Valley when they arrived." This descendant also wrote about Sarah's love for little children and how she always had little gifts for them:

"Whenever we left her home after a visit with her she would always give us some food to eat on the way, should we become hungry. We always remember the large pockets in her long skirts, and in her aprons, where we could always find some nice candy or a cookie. She was dearly loved by all. Every memory we have of her, every thought and action was a pleasant one."[2]

According to one line of Sarah's descendants, the shawl was returned to Sarah at some point and is in their possession today. Stories regarding the retrieval of Sarah's shawl, who returned it to Sarah, and whether or not George's body was still there have to my knowledge not been documented. In *17 Miracles,* T. C. refers to the "taking up" of George's body as simply the speculation of some.

Concerning the Indian-style burial of George Padley, there is ample evidence that the pioneers had witnessed such things along the trail, particularly near Fort Laramie. The Martin handcart company had passed the Fort Laramie area on October 10, about a month before George Padley died. Mary Barton of the Martin company recorded what she saw there:

"We found Indians wrapped in blankets and laid across the boughs of trees. This was another form of burial the Indians had for their dead."[3]

Other diarists and record keepers from other years reported the same thing within a day's travel of Fort Laramie:

"Monday, Sep14 [1863]

"Started this morning at 7—30, *passed [Fort]* Laramie about 10 . . . crossed the river about 11 miles above Laramie. . . . camped on the South side.

"Tuesday Sep 15 [1863]

"Shortly after leaving camp on a high tree on the edge of a high cliff, we noticed the dead body of an Indian wrapped in his blanket & strapped to the branches of the tree. That being his burial place. It was said he was there last year."[4]

The Willie handcart company journal-keeper noted this same area as they passed it on September 29: "Left Camp about 8 A.M., passed an Indian Agency Station where some Sioux Indians were camped. Nooned at a vacant Trading Post 7 miles from Fort Laramie and camped for the night on the road near an Indian Burying Ground about 4 miles from that Fort with weeds and young cottonwood for the cattle."[5]

The Martin handcart company passed the same Indian burial ground less than two weeks after the Willie company.

It may be the one described by Mary Ann Barton of the Martin company. Mary Ann was 14 years old at the time.

The worries associated with wolves digging up graves along the pioneer trail was a problem for all travelers, not just the late 1856 companies. In returning from his service in the Mormon Battalion, Levi Savage served as a subcaptain in the larger group captained by Levi Ward Hancock (1803–1881). Levi Hancock was a musician and poet in the Battalion. In early December 1847, the Battalion reached the ruins of the Rancho San Bernardino, where one of their members, Elisha Smith, died and was buried. It is said that the howls of large wolves made that night hideous, and Levi Hancock composed the song "Death of the Wolves," a version of which was sung by many pioneers afterward.[6]

It is not known if the members of the Willie or Martin handcart companies knew or sang this song, but they certainly experienced the distress caused by the wolves howling at night and digging up graves.

A story that might have been comforting for Sarah Franks and others was told at the funeral of President Jedediah M. Grant, counselor to President Brigham Young, just a few days after the arrival of the Martin handcart company in the Salt Lake Valley. President Grant had traveled to the Salt Lake Valley in the fall of 1847. As his company neared Independence Rock and Devil's Gate, his wife, Caroline, became very sick and was expected to die. The Grants' three-month-old baby, Margaret, did die at this time and was buried in a shallow grave. Caroline couldn't bear the thought of wolves ravaging her baby's grave and begged Jedediah to return to the baby's gravesite and take her body to Salt Lake to be buried next to her own. Caroline died after arriving in Salt Lake, and Jedediah immediately traveled back on the plains to keep his promise to his wife. Upon arriving at the baby's gravesite, he was horrified to witness the desecration of the grave by wolves. For nine long years, Jedediah grieved over being too late to keep his promise to Caroline.

When the Martin company arrived in Salt Lake City on November 30, 1856, President Grant was extremely ill with pneumonia. He had his attendants raise him to the window by his bedside so he could wave to the people arriving in the Valley. He died the next day.

President Heber C. Kimball spoke at the funeral a few days later and told the large audience of the visits of Jedediah M. Grant to the spirit world a short time before:

"I went to see him [Jedediah M. Grant] one day last week, and he reached out his hand and shook hands with me; he could not speak, but he shook hands warmly with me. I felt for him, and wanted to raise him up, and to have him stay and help us whip the devils and bring to pass righteousness. Why? Because he was valiant, and I loved him. He was a great help to us, and you would be, if you were as valiant as he was, which you can be through faithfulness and obedience.

"I laid my hands upon him and blessed him, and asked God to strengthen his lungs that he might be easier, and in two or three minutes he raised himself up and talked for about an hour as busily as he could, telling me what he had seen and what he understood, until I was afraid he would weary himself, when I arose and left him.

"He said to me, brother Heber, I have been into the spirit world two nights in succession, and, of all the dreads that ever came across me, the worst was to have to again return to my body, though I had to do it. . . .

"He saw the righteous gathered together in the spirit world, and there were no wicked spirits among them. He saw his wife; she was the first person that came to him. He saw many that he knew, but did not have conversation with any except his wife, Caroline. She came to him, and he said that she looked beautiful and had their little child, that died on the Plains, in her arms, and said, 'Mr. Grant, here is little Margaret; you know that the wolves ate her up, but it did not hurt her; here she is all right.'"[7]

Although President Grant did not receive this comforting vision regarding the burial of his baby until nine years after the event, surely his publicly related experience was a comfort to those entering the Valley and hearing it that very week. Gibson Condie, one of the rescuers, attended President Grant's funeral and wrote about it. He said that President Grant's "wonderful vision of those two nights was listened to with rapt attention by the large Audience and was repeated for years after by many who heard it. . . . he was mourned by thousands and left in their memories a name that will be forever [honored] throughout the Territory."[8]

Not only was Sarah Franks' shawl a symbol of the love she and George had for each other but it was a symbol of Sarah's mother's trust in George to get her daughter to the Valley safely.

15

Did any miracles happen during the filming of 17 Miracles*?*

T. C.: Yes! In the film, we tell the love story of George Padley and Sarah Franks. They are sweethearts but have decided to wait until they get to Zion to be married. To help tell their story, I wanted them to have an affectionate gesture that would signal their love for each other. In talking about that idea with actors Natalie Blackman and Jason Celaya, we came up with the idea that at certain moments in the film, such as when they first see each other or part from each other, each would lightly touch his or her own heart with their fingers.

After George has suffered through terrible conditions, carried others through the freezing Platte River, and given his meager rations to Sarah, he succumbs and dies. We were out in Utah's west desert when we filmed their final, tender scene together, in which Sarah says good-bye and leaves George's burial site. It was sunset. Natalie did a great job and recited her lines wonderfully. I felt great about the scene as I drove home that night until it hit me—we had forgotten to have her give the love sign! It was in the script, and yet no one on the set had caught the omission.

I was sick. I had to have that love sign. The biggest problems were that the snow had melted that day, we had Natalie only one more day before she was leaving to live in Boston, and we were not scheduled to go back out to the west desert. I arrived home and groused to my wife about it. She thought about it and said, "Here's what you do. Get Natalie to come to your next location, put the camera low and shoot up so you don't see the ground. Have her do just that part of the scene. Cut it in, and no one will know."

The next day we had Natalie arrive on set a bit early. We were in a completely different location, and there was no snow on the ground. But we set the camera a little low, looking up into the sky so we wouldn't see the ground. We matched Natalie's costume and appearance from the earlier shoot and did a take. I didn't like it. I wasn't feeling it. I didn't think Natalie was feeling it. It certainly didn't help that when we filmed the original scene on the west desert, she played the scene while looking at George's body in the tree. Now she only had a marker to play to.

We did a second take—no good. A third take—also not right. I tried changing the dialogue. It just wasn't what it needed to be. Take four—I didn't feel good about it, and on and on we went until we got to take eight, and on take eight, Natalie nailed it. She emoted that deep feeling of love for George and said her lines perfectly. I was thrilled. And just as she was saying, "I love you, George Padley. It will all be worth it," a flock of geese flew through the frame, and I don't mean just somewhere in the background. If I had been able to say, "Exactly here is where I want the geese to enter frame and exactly right now," I wouldn't have done it any differently.

Then as Sarah touched her heart and turned to leave George, a second flock of geese flew through the frame. (We added the sound of the honking geese in the audio track.)

I love that scene. It was perfect. The geese bring into the scene an idea beyond death, an idea of moving on, just going to another place. I don't even care now about the touching of the heart. The geese are to me what that scene is all about. It was only through a series of seemingly unfortunate events that we were finally given the added texture and meaning to the scene.

Jolene: Just as with the pioneers' stories, all the scenes are my favorites. When I've asked my grandchildren and others which scene they like best, I've gotten many different answers. Some of them like Albert's comical character and "superb" lines. Some like Louisa Mellor and her mother's story of the pie. I hadn't thought of choosing a favorite scene until a friend told me her only complaint about the movie—she was quite disappointed that there was not a kiss between Sarah and George. When she told me that, I realized I hadn't even noticed. Each time I've seen the movie since then, I've marveled at how T. C. could get away with such a thing, given the standard of movies in today's world.

The scene where George and Sarah are shown having tender moments together is definitely one of my favorites. I love how they run and laugh and play as the emotions between them build to the point of George longing to kiss Sarah. She longs for it, too, but recognizes the need to gently check the building passions that might cause them to fail to achieve their goal of being sealed in Zion. A kiss would have not been inappropriate in the movie, but I loved T. C.'s portrayal of George's reluctant restraint in accordance with Sarah's wishes.

16

Was the river crossing depicted in the film the one we've heard about in which three young men carried all the company members across?

T. C.: When I began my research for writing the script, I made a point of talking to several Latter-day Saint historians. The first advice they gave me was, "Don't fall into the Sweetwater trap." I said, "Okay, what's the Sweetwater trap?" They wouldn't tell me. They just said to get into the research and I would figure it out.

I did figure it out. They were warning me that some of the stories we have heard for many years regarding the incident of rescuer boys carrying others across the Sweetwater are incomplete and therefore reflect some historical inaccuracies. Chad M. Orton wrote about this event in a paper for *BYU Studies,* from which I learned a great deal.[1]

There were other tough, cold, river crossings, and I wanted to be sure to include one in the film. I decided to make it the last crossing of the North Platte, which the Martin company undertook on October 19. That was before any of the rescuers had made their way to them. But it still had all the drama of the icy river, and though all of the Saints were exhausted and starving at this point, many helped others get across, notably Sarah Ann Haigh, who is remembered for making several trips back and forth, carrying others. She is represented in the film by actress Tara Oldroyd, who carries another girl on her back across the river.

Of course the main point of the river crossing scene is that it leads to the death of George Padley. By this time

George would have been giving much of his food to Sarah (and perhaps others) for quite a while. He was exhausted and starving and now had to endure this terrible ordeal.

When I first shot the scene, I did not have George fall into the water. We cut the scene, and it was very good, very dramatic, but when I showed that version to a few teenagers, some of them asked, "Why did George die not long after that? Why was that such a big deal? Why couldn't they have gotten across, built a fire, dried out, gotten warm, and just moved on?"

Unless we have experienced similar conditions ourselves, I don't think we can begin to fathom what it was like for those pioneers to be 300 miles from anywhere when they crossed the Platte for the last time. It's zero degrees when you get soaked by icy water, and then your clothes freeze to your skin. Without any way to get warm, hypothermia sets in, which even for healthy, well-fed persons would be enough to cause death. Some of the pioneers had been undernourished before, but added to that was the energy they had expended on the trek, not just walking but pushing and pulling a handcart, day after day, week after week, with little to eat. Imagine George having only thin, worn clothes to wear and being weakened further by having given much of his meager rations to others. That he would die under those conditions is not at all farfetched. In truth, it would almost be expected. But having him soaked and chilled would make the reason for his death even more plain.

So we went back and added that additional moment of George tripping and going under the water with the woman on his back. After that, there was no having to explain why George died from the effects of the ordeal.

Jolene: Several accounts of that fateful crossing of the Platte River on October 19 were recorded by members of the Martin handcart company. Among them is one by Sarah Ann Haigh, who at age 19 crossed the river numerous times, helping other members of the company. When I first reviewed the unfinished film, T. C. asked excitedly, "Did you notice I got Sarah Haigh in there?" I was pleased that Sarah's heroic efforts are memorialized in the film. Just thinking about her ordeal and her selfless service fills me with wonder and admiration.

Other members of the Martin company wrote detailed accounts of the October 19th crossing of the Platte River. A published account of several river crossings, including those of the Platte written by Martin company member John Jaques, was available as early as 1878 in the *Salt Lake Daily Herald.* Part of his record is quoted in *17 Miracles:*

"Platte crossing, Oct. 19: That was a bitter cold day. Winter came on all at once, and that was the first day of it. The river was wide, the current strong, the water exceedingly cold and up to the wagon beds in the deepest parts, and the bed of the river was covered with cobble stones. Some of the men carried some of the women over on their backs or in their arms, but others of the women tied up their skirts and waded through, like heroines as they were, and as they had done through many other rivers and creeks. The company was barely over when snow, hail, and sleet began to fall, accompanied by a piercing north wind, and camp was made on this side of the river."[2]

Charlotte Mellor, who was 14 at the time, captured the dreadful experience of October 19 in these words: "On entering the water, our first impulse was to turn back and not wade across. The water was so cold that it sent pains right to the bone and the muscles cramped. We steadied ourselves as we held on to the cart and pushed. Father pulled. By the time we got across, our limbs were so numb that we could hardly keep from falling as we trudged along. The north wind cut like a sharp knife."[3]

Likewise, 16-year-old Albert Jones recorded another result of the last crossing of the Platte: "At the first fall of snow, fell a great gloom upon the camp, a dread and fear came upon us—we boys that up to this date rendered attentions to the girls had our spirits checked to freezing point and the little god Cupid sped off for warmer climes."[4]

Despite the difficulties of the Platte River crossing on October 19, it has not received as much attention as the later and more widely remembered crossing of the Sweetwater River on November 4. But it was a severe ordeal that caused much suffering, and many sacrifices were made by members of the Martin, Hodgetts, and Hunt companies alike.

An account of the Sweetwater crossing by Solomon Kimball has through various means become quite well known to Church members:

"Three eighteen-year-old boys belonging to the relief party came to the rescue; and to the astonishment of all who saw, carried nearly every member of that ill-fated handcart company across the snow-bound stream. The strain was so terrible, and the exposure so great, that in later years all the boys died from the effects of it. When President Brigham Young heard of this heroic act, he wept like a child, and later declared publicly, 'That act alone will ensure C. Allen Huntington, George W. Grant, and David P. Kimball an everlasting salvation in the Celestial Kingdom of God, worlds without end.'"[5]

That this one well-known and often-quoted paragraph is incomplete and has some inaccuracies, such as the ages of the three named young men and what President Brigham Young really said, has not made it any less inspiring when the focus is the rescuers' sacrifice in saving the lives of others.[6]

Several members of the Martin handcart company wrote about their crossing of the Sweetwater on November

4, in which rescuers spent a long time in the water carrying others across the river. Some gave the names of from one to four of these men—George W. Grant, David P. Kimball, Stephen W. Taylor, and Clark Allen Huntington. Research by modern historian Chad Orton (mentioned earlier by T. C.) has identified Ira Nebeker as an additional rescuer, and it is believed that there were likely more, although they remain unnamed. Orton discusses health problems that affected these four young men. Additional recent research identifies statements about Clark Allen Huntington, who was 24 years old at the time of the rescue and died in 1896 at the age of 64.

Frank Johnson, to whom Huntington served as a surrogate father when Frank's father broke his back and became an invalid, recorded: "Clark Allen suffered from severe coughing spells for most of his life. These spells started after his experience of carrying the Martin Handcart Saints across the Sweet Water River in Wyoming in 1856."[7]

Alexander Wiley Huntington, a son of Clark Huntington who was with his father much of the time during the last three years of his father's life, recalled: "[Father] contracted a cough when he had helped the people at the Sweetwater and it stayed with him all the rest of his life, eventually causing his death."[8]

Two brief personal accounts that have also become well-known among members of the Church are from Ellen

("Nellie") Pucell and Francis Webster, who were members of the Martin company. The terrible October 19 Platte River crossing depicted in *17 Miracles* led directly to the death of both parents of 10-year-old Nellie and to the amputation of her lower legs.

Nellie's parents, Samuel and Margaret Pucell, were among the first converts to the LDS Church in England. If our information is correct, Margaret was the second woman baptized into the Church there. She and Samuel gave the first sixpence the Mormon elders received while laboring in the Preston area. For nineteen years the Pucell family scrimped and saved so they could escape their poverty and persecution and join the Saints in Zion. During this time they continued to entertain the missionaries in their small home. It is said that sometimes their children went to bed hungry in order to provide a meal for the missionaries.

Several years after Nellie's arrival in Utah, she married William Unthank and gave birth to six children. Most of the information about Nellie that we are familiar with comes from an account written by William Palmer entitled "She Stood Tall on Her Knees." Excerpts from this article give great insight into the way Nellie handled her disability the rest of her life:

"In poverty and pain she reared a family of six children but never asked for favors of pity or charity because of her tragic handicap. William was a poor man and unable to provide fully for his family; so Nellie did all she could for herself. She took in washings. Kneeling by a tub on the floor she scrubbed the clothes to whiteness on the washboard. She knit stockings to sell, carded wool, and crocheted table pieces. She seldom accepted gifts or charity from friends or neighbors unless she could do a bundle of darning or mending to repay the kindness.

"The bishop and the Relief Society sometimes gave a little assistance which Nellie gratefully accepted, but once a year, to even the score, she took her children and cleaned the meetinghouse. The boys carried water, the girls washed the windows, and Nellie, on her knees, scrubbed the floor.

"This heroic woman gave to William Unthank a posterity to perpetuate his name in the earth and he gave her a home and a family to give comfort and care in her old age.

"In memory I recall her wrinkled forehead, her soft dark eyes that told of toil and pain and suffering, and the deep grooves that encircled the corners of her strong mouth. But in that face there was no trace of bitterness or railings at her fate. There was patience and serenity for in spite of her handicap she had earned her keep and justified her existence. She had given more to family, friends and to the world than she had received."[9]

The family of Josiah Rogerson, a 15-year-old boy in the

Martin handcart company, cared for the Pucell orphans, Nellie and Margaret, after they arrived in Salt Lake City. Josiah later wrote a series of articles about the handcart migration for the *Salt Lake Herald* in 1907, including the following excerpt:

"One morning while at the Buttes [October 23–27] the wife of Samuel Pucell, about 55 or 60 years of age, from the Ashton-under-Lyne Branch, Lancashire, England, came to our tent and, pushing aside the cloth door, said, calling to my mother: 'Mary, our Sam's (her husband) dead, and I'll not be long after him. When I'm dee-ad, do thee take care of my two lassies after thou gets to the Valley, and be a good mother to 'em. I'll not reach there.' No words of mother could cheer her up, or dispel her conclusion. The next morning afterward . . . she had gone to her Sam. . . . The two daughters, Margaret and Helen [Ellen] went with my mother to Parowan, Iron County, Utah, the same winter, and have been residents of Cedar City, Utah, for the last forty-five years, and well known as Mrs. John Walker and Mrs. Unthanks [Unthank]. Their mother and father, just referred to, were among the first members of the Preston branch of the church, Lancashire, England, organized there in July, 1837, by President Heber C. Kimball and others, and I have it from my mother that Sister Pucell (I think her name was Margaret) at one time, hearing that some of the six or eight associate elders of President

Kimball hadn't anything to eat one day, took one of her skirts and pawned it for enough to buy a loaf of bread, a few ounces of tea and sugar, and half a pound of butter, which she took to the elders, begging them to accept the donation. The youngest daughter, Helen [Ellen], of the Pucell family, then about 12 [10] years of age, arrived in Salt Lake with her feet so badly frozen that both were amputated soon afterward. Of such Saints and graduates in the primitive love of the gospel was Captain Edward Martin's handcart company composed."[10]

Francis Webster is another handcart pioneer who has become widely known among Church members, though not generally by his name. He was "the old man" who stood up in a Sunday School class, chastised the other class members for criticizing the Church and its leaders about the Martin handcart company tragedy, and spoke of angels pushing his handcart, of the price he willingly paid to reach Zion, and of those who likewise suffered but did not leave the Church. His inspiring testimony regarding his travel in the Martin handcart company still rings in our ears today:

"Was I sorry that I chose to come by handcart? No. Neither then nor any minute of my life since. The price we paid to become acquainted with God was a privilege to pay, and I am thankful that I was privileged to come in the Martin Handcart Company."[11]

17

Was Captain James G. Willie really as harsh as he is depicted when Levi Savage spoke out against continuing the journey that season?

T. C.: Paul Willie, one of Captain James G. Willie's descendants, said of him, "He was a man of implicit trust and faith and told those who wanted to stay behind that 'he wanted no naysayers' in the company." On several occasions he chided the people for bickering and not strictly following the company rules and at one point dismissed Johan Ahmanson as subcaptain over a contingent of Danish Saints. I sense that Captain Willie recognized that it was absolutely essential that everyone be in step or the company would fall apart in disaster. I don't believe he was a tyrant, but he knew that strong leadership and unity were essential to the venture.

The words spoken by Levi Savage in the film, expressing his view that the company should not continue on that late in the season, come directly from pioneer journals and later writings.

There are at least three points to consider about Captain Willie's response.

First, pioneer companies were organized along military lines, as evidenced by the calling of a "captain" to lead a "company" of Saints. To ensure the success of the difficult endeavor, leaders needed to keep the participants on task during their journey.

Second, Captain Willie knew the risky situation the company was in, but he also knew what would happen if a schism developed. If doubt crept in and many decided not to continue westward, he would have chaos on his hands. I believe that was part of his strong response—an attempt at unification by saying, in effect, "I am in charge here; no dissenters are needed."

Third, and probably most important, it was a different time. It is easy for us to stand back more than 150 years later and make judgments, but being called to repentance in front of an entire congregation was not uncommon in those days. Today, it would be completely inappropriate, but that's not how it was back then.

It is obvious from the writings of many in the Willie company that Captain Willie was regarded as a great and giving leader—a man ready to lay down his life for those he served. And after reading what they had to say about him, I believe he was a kind, loving, Christlike man who had been given a very difficult assignment and who tried his best to meet the challenge.

Jolene: Before the emigration, while still on his mission in his native England and not knowing he would be called to captain a handcart company on his way back to Utah, James G. Willie wrote in his missionary diary: "November 25, 1855, Sunday . . . in the afternoon I attended the meeting at ½ past 2 and partook of the Holy Sacrament, after which I addressed the meeting upon the necessity of being humble and childlike in our natures, and so prepare when the way shall open for us to emigrate that we might not lose our faith in the promises of God while journeying to the vallies of the mountains. I also spoke some on emigration matters and the necessity of living acceptable before God, thus proving our faith by our works."[1]

I have seen nothing but praise for Captain James G. Willie from the members of his company. George Cunningham, who was 15 at the time of the events, later wrote:

"Our Captain showed us all a noble example. He was furnished a mule to ride on our start from Iowa City, but he said, 'I will never get on its back. I will show the example, you follow it.' He did so and the Captains of hundreds followed him. They would crowd on ahead to be the first into the streams to help the women and children across. They waded every stream, I might say, a dozen times between Iowa City and Green River. . . . Their feet were worn and bleeding, they became exhausted and had to be hauled the balance of the way, some of them not being able to stand on their feet."[2]

The Willie company journal records the following just one week before reaching the Valley:

"November 2, 1856—Bros. Willie, Woodward, & Christiansen stayed behind to bring up the sick. This morning we had not teams enough to haul the feeble that were left behind. After a short time several teams came on from the Valley & picked up the sick. The brethren that stayed behind were late into camp. . . . Bro. Willie's feet were in such a bad condition from frost that he was unable to walk to the Camp; a wagon was sent for him."[3]

On October 20, the Willie company's progress ground to a halt. They were out of food and dealing with their first snowstorm. James Willie and Joseph Elder left the company and went on a risky horseback ride of more than 20 miles in search of the rescue party. Their search took them across the area known as Rocky Ridge. Of that search for help, Joseph Elder recorded, "The snow and an awful cold wind blew in our faces all day."[4]

Upon reaching the rescue party camp, they turned around and went back, bringing help and hope to the stranded handcart company. Two days later, James Willie crossed Rocky Ridge again, this time with his company. When it was close to midnight and all of his people had not yet reached camp, he headed back out on the trail to find them. Such was the devotion and leadership of James Willie.

As a result of his continuing service to his company members, Captain Willie's feet were badly frostbitten. Upon James's arrival in the Valley a doctor recommended amputation. Due in part to devoted nursing by his wife, Elizabeth Pettit Willie, James was blessed to keep his feet.

Another little known act of charity by James Willie occurred while he was still on his mission in England. James had a brother, John, who had died a few years before. The estate was finally settled, and James inherited a fairly large sum of money. He used only a small amount to defray his mission expenses and gave the rest, about £200, to the Perpetual Emigration Fund to pay for the passage of many emigrants.

The seeming harshness portrayed in the movie by James Willie was not unusual behavior for leaders endeavoring to move hundreds of people and cattle across a thousand miles of wilderness in about three months. Strict obedience and unity were essential to the safety and success of the company. It required the collective positive efforts and attitudes of all. Even before leaving Iowa City, James Willie had received counsel from immigration agents about how to discipline the company. Levi Savage recorded a day the company did not move because of that counsel:

"Camp of the Saints, Thurs. 17th July 1856. Today we remained in camp. Evening we held meeting. Brother Willie gave good instructions, also rehearsed the counsel that

Brother Spencer left for the Saints; which was not to move off this ground, until the spirit of murmuring, if there was any, ceased among the Saints of this camp. A good spirit prevailed."[5]

Levi Savage seems to have had an honest and blunt personality. The incident in the film in which he speaks his mind concerning the journey was not unusual for him. Judging from several other diary entries, Levi spoke out similarly at other times in his life. Yet once he had made his opinions known, he was always willing to humbly follow the counsel of his leaders and publicly repent if needed.

A tender tribute was given by Mary Hurren Wight, who was 8 years old when she traveled in the Willie company: "Captain [James G.] Willie was in charge of our company. He had been in England on a mission and was returning to his family in Utah. We all loved Captain Willie. He was kind and considerate, and did all that he could for the comfort of those in his company. Many times he has laid his hands upon my head and administered to me.

"I remember my father lived at Hyde Park at the time of the death of Bro. Willie. He had not heard of his sickness and he cried when he heard of his death. He said that if he had known that he had been sick he would willingly have walked from Hyde Park to Mendon to see him if need be."[6]

18

Was Albert a real person? If so, what can you tell us about him?

T. C.: I was so fortunate a few years ago to have met Travis Eberhard, the man who plays the part of Albert in the film. Travis works as a film editor. He is a very distinctive person—happy, upbeat, and completely self-reliant. When I first read of the unnamed disabled pioneer in *The Price We Paid,*[1] I knew he'd be a great movie character, and I immediately thought of Travis. We got him to come in for a casting session. He was already doing a pretty good English accent and wanted the role, but one thing stood in the way: Travis had never really walked, and the character of Albert was determined to walk to Zion.

Bruce Wing, our great property master, made some rustic crutches for Travis. We took them to him at his apartment. Travis practiced for a few weeks and was soon able to get around pretty well with them. To further the illusion, when we filmed Travis walking, as in the race with Buffalo Chip Boy, I ran the camera at a slower speed and had the background people walk in slow motion. This resulted in Travis's seeming to go faster than he actually was, and it kept the audience from thinking that he'd never be able to walk 100 feet, let alone all the way to Zion. Since the DVD was released, I have done many signings with Travis. He is everyone's favorite. As soon as he gets there, I become wallpaper. Everyone wants to talk to him, especially children. That is as it should be. Travis is a great person and just naturally attracts people to want to get to know him and be around him.

Jolene: The character portrayed as Albert in the movie was based on an actual member of the Martin handcart company, described by fellow traveler John William Southwell. He did not give the man's name in his account, so T. C. assigned the name Albert to the character. Southwell wrote:

"In [the] company was one of the worst cripples I ever saw to be a traveler. His lower limbs were paralyzed and his body badly deformed but he was strong in the faith. He was able to propel himself with surprising speed with the use of crutches.

"On the road the [company] missed him. The road followed down an old dry bed of a creek but finally crossed on to the other side where we expected to get back of him. There were, on the road he was traveling, faint tracks that had been used by stock, perhaps buffalo, and the poor fellow followed those tracks instead of crossing on the other side. We camped for noon near the loup part of the Platte River. Myself and two other men, taking a hand cart, went back to where we left the buffalo tracks and followed down about a mile when to our horror we saw around an old tree two large gray wolves prowling around, and half a dozen eagles hovering over the tree waiting for him to quit his screams and gesticulations with his crutches so they could pounce upon him and devour him in his cramped position under the roots of the tree, screaming out his death knell.

"We arrived in time to save him from his pending fate, took him out and placed him on the cart we had brought, placed him in position to ride back to camp. How the poor fellow begged us to let him walk, as he said he had promised Brother [Daniel] Tyler when we started on our trip that he would walk every foot of the way to Salt Lake City. However, we only saved him to travel a few days longer, when at the close of the sixth day's march his trouble in this world came to an end and he was buried on the banks of the Elkhorn River where one other passed beyond the veil of tears."[2]

I had searched for the identity of this man for some time, trying to discover who had died when the Martin company was traveling near the Loup part of the Platte River. I found other Martin company diarists who wrote of the crippled man who was lost. They all gave a confirming date, but like Southwell, did not name him.

James G. Bleak. "Friday 12th We travelled but 6 miles, in consequence of it being discovered that a cripple had been left behind."[3]

Samuel Openshaw. "Sept. 12—Started about 8 o'clock, traveled about 4 miles when we came to the Wood River which we crossed on a small bridge yankee; continued down the side of it, stopped for dinner at 12 o'clock. For ought we knew, but a cripple, a young man who walked with crutches, had been left behind. We sent four men back to search for him, which caused us to move none today. About sunset they brought him into the camp."[4]

William Binder. "Friday Sept. 12th: The weather was excessively hot today. The company was detained today through a cripple stopping behind and only travelled 7 miles."[5]

About the time T. C. was finalizing the film in 2011, I obtained from the Church History Library a copy of *Life History and Writings of John Jaques,* by Stella Jaques Bell. Years before, I had borrowed a copy of the book from Jaques descendants and returned it to them shortly afterwards. I had used it only for writing the brief Jaques family biographies for my stake's handcart trek in 2000. I may have noticed the following journal entry, but if so, it didn't mean anything to me then.

John Jaques. "Fri. 12 [September 12, 1856]: Left camp about 8 A.M. In about three miles crossed Wood River after crossing a dry creek with steep banks, taking the cattle off the wagons to cross both. Kept along side of the river for five miles and baited. Robert Pearce was missing and several men were sent out with a handcart to find him. This detained the company here for the night. He had gone up the side of Wood River instead of crossing it."[6]

Here at last was the name of the man who had been identified only as "crippled" by four other diarists in the Martin company—"Robert Pearce"! A short time later I was looking through another book I had read but forgotten—*Miracles of the Martin Handcart Company,* by JoAnn Mellor Felix. JoAnn had identified this man as Robert Pierce (or Pearce). If I had referred to that book first, T. C.'s movie would have used the correct name. As it was, I called T. C. and told him of my discovery in time for him to add in a postscript to the movie that the real name of the crippled character, Albert, was not discovered until after filming was complete. His name was actually Robert Pierce.

The search continues for more information about Robert Pierce, but a few things are known: Robert Pierce was 31 years old when he left England in 1856. The British Mission Record (BMR) at the Church History Library shows Robert Pierce's address when he signed up to travel on the ship *Horizon* in April 1856 as "Jn Kay L'Pool." "L'Pool" is an abbreviation of Liverpool. The BMR also shows Pierce was in the Liverpool Conference allotment of emigrants for this ship. "Jn Kay," it seems, was the missionary Elder John Moburn Kay, who was serving in the Liverpool Branch early in 1856. The reference to Elder Kay likely indicates that he was to receive Robert Pierce's *Horizon* ticket.

John Jaques's diary entry for January 8, 1856, indicates that Elder Kay was with him on the day that copies of the

Deseret News arrived in Liverpool. That newspaper contained a copy of the recently released official "Epistle" announcing the plan for emigrant Saints to travel by handcart rather than by wagon. Brother Jaques wrote:

"Tues. 8: The Utah November mail came in, bringing 'Deseret News' No. 30 to 34, the last number containing the Thirteenth General Epistle of the First Presidency. About 8 o'clock P.M. went with my wife, and her sister, Tamar, and my daughter, Flora Loader [Jaques], to Elder George Tumbull's, Miss Margaret Aison Fait having been married to him on the 2nd instant. Flora, being unwell, was rather peevish. Elders George D. Grant, John Kay, William H. Kimball, Spicer W. Crandall, Asa Calkins, Thomas Williams, and James Linforth and wife, and Brother William Perks were present. Spent a very pleasant evening. Left for home at 12½."[7]

A Daughters of Utah Pioneers history for John Moburn Kay praises him as a champion of the underdog. He may have been the elder who baptized Robert Pierce.

Robert Pierce's occupation is identified in the British Mission Record as "Pedlar." Imagine what Robert's hopes and dreams might have been as he contemplated leaving behind his peddling of wares on the streets of Liverpool for a new life in the Rocky Mountains. No wonder he was willing to "walk" the 1,300 miles to get there.

Robert was not the only disabled handcart pioneer in

the 1856 companies. Peder Mortensen had been well-to-do in Denmark and endured severe persecution when he joined the Church. Unable to walk, Peder and his daughter Annie Kirstine (Steena) of the Willie company were pulled in the two family handcarts for more than a thousand miles. Nevertheless, they assisted with the migration in every way possible. Steena sewed tents and wagon covers until her fingers were raw. She helped her mother prepare burial coverings for the dead at Rock Creek, donating precious family linens she had helped weave in Denmark.[8]

Thomas Kirkwood of the Willie company was likewise a traveler in the family handcart, which was pulled by Margaret Kirkwood, his widowed mother, and Robert, his brother.[9]

In the Martin handcart company with Robert Pierce were the orphaned sisters Charlotte and Betsy Mee. Like Robert Pierce, Charlotte had a great determination to reach Zion at all costs. She wrote:

"When I was seventeen years old [1853], I sprained or broke some of the ligaments in my ankle and the doctor said I must lose my leg, but I refused to have it amputated. I was forced to use crutches for nearly four years. With my fourteen-year-old sister, I set sail for America on May 25th, 1856, on the ship *Horizon* under Captain Reed. . . . From Iowa, we came by handcart. Part of the way I walked, and part of the way I was hauled in a wagon or handcart. One day I walked and crawled eight miles, and my knees finally bled. We had a very hard trip. . . . The next month [after reaching the Salt Lake Valley] my ankle was operated upon and the year following I was baptized for my health and was able to walk soon after."[10]

19

Did Levi Savage really have anything to do with the Donner Party?

T. C.: The research I found and the Donner expert I consulted during preproduction did not state which of the two groups of discharged Mormon Battalion members traveling from California over the Sierra Nevada Levi was in. For artistic reasons, I decided to put him with General Stephen W. Kearny because it gave me two things: first, Levi's exposure to a pioneering tragedy that would provide a continuing theme in the film, and second, it was a way to establish Levi's character by contrasting his reverence for life and his belief in prayer with General Kearny's perhaps more hardened view. But even the second group of Mormon Battalion veterans found much carnage and had to dispose of human remains. So, whichever group Levi was in, he experienced the aftermath of pioneering tragedies. Remember that *17 Miracles* is not a documentary; it is instead a dramatic story based on true experiences.

Jolene: As discharged members of the 1846–47 Mormon Battalion, Levi Savage and many of the others returned east in 1847 on pioneer trails. They were anxious to meet the exiled Mormons they had left the previous year in Council Bluffs, Iowa, where Battalion members had received their orders from Brigadier General Stephen W. Kearny, commander of the U.S. Army of the West.

In late May 1847, General Kearny began a march out of California to Fort Leavenworth, Kansas, where he was taking Lieutenant Colonel John C. Fremont to begin court-martial proceedings. Kearny had ordered 15 men from the Mormon Battalion to serve as escorts to this contingent. Levi Savage was *not* among those 15 men.

In mid-June, Kearny's group found two cabins used by the Donner party the previous winter. The men called these places the "cannibal camps." Kearny detailed five Battalion members and Major Thomas Swords to bury the bodies that remained and then to burn the first cabin, as depicted in *17 Miracles.* Battalion member Matthew Caldwell wrote that they buried the human remains in "an old cellar" before setting fire to the cabin. A mile farther down the trail they came to a second cabin and more bodies, but General Kearny did not order these to be buried or burned.

Kearny's contingent met the first group of Mormon pioneers heading westward in July at Independence Rock, about 50 miles west of present-day Casper, Wyoming.

Thirteen of the 15 Mormon Battalion members arrived at Fort Leavenworth on August 23, 1847. The next day they were given clothing and severance pay and traveled to Council Bluffs, Iowa, where they had begun their journey the previous summer.

Meanwhile, back in Los Angeles, California, the rest of the Mormon Battalion members were officially discharged on July 16, 1847. Of that group, 79 men chose to reenlist; 5 returned on the southern trail they had just blazed; 4 chose to remain in California; 6 others stayed to work for Isaac Williams, building a mill at his ranch near Los Angeles; and the rest left California, headed north under the leadership of Levi Hancock. Levi Savage served as a captain of 10 in this group of more than 200 men. Upon reaching the Cosumnes Valley near Sutter's Fort, the soldiers learned that Brigham Young and the Mormon pioneers were settling in the Great Salt Lake Valley. A dozen men decided to remain in the area and obtain work at Sutter's Fort and other places. It was here that Levi Savage and his comrades heard firsthand accounts of the fate of the Donner Party from John P. Rhoades, who had been with the rescue parties sent out to bring in the surviving members of that party.

Levi Savage and the other returning soldiers left their camp at Johnson's Ranch on August 29, 1847, and followed the same trail General Kearny had taken several weeks before. When they reached the Sierra Nevada Mountains, they received a letter from Brigham Young advising all those with families to stay in California and work for one year. About half the men returned to Sutter's Fort to find employment, leaving approximately 100 men to continue to Salt Lake. Levi Savage was among those who continued east and were horrified at the sight of what was left of the "cannibal camp" when they found it. Although Levi was apparently not keeping a diary at this time, other members of this group were, and they described in detail the terrible scene. Ricketts wrote, in summary, "The soldiers thought it was a scene of intense suffering as well as fiendish acts and were relieved to leave the tragic camp."[1]

The first group of former Mormon Battalion soldiers arrived in the Salt Lake Valley on October 16, 1847, and 29 of them continued east to meet their families at Winter Quarters on the Missouri River. Levi Savage stayed in the Valley, so he was not with those men but he would have known them. They included Reddick N. Allred (rescuer), Edward Bunker (captain, third handcart company), and Daniel Tyler (counselor and subcaptain in the Martin handcart company). Journeying east in 1847, these men suffered greatly from lack of provisions and snowstorms as they broke trail through deep snow for hundreds of miles and nearly died from cold and starvation. After one river crossing they ate some of their horses that had drowned in the crossing. They became so destitute that they even ate rawhide from their saddle bags.

In his autobiography, Levi summarized leaving Winter Quarters for service in the Battalion, his arrival in the Salt Lake Valley over a year later, and his subsequent mission call, which brought him back to the United States in time to assist the Willie handcart company:

"We left our friends in their wagons in a wild Indian country. Our enlistment dates from the 16th of July 1846. We marched on foot . . . to Los Angeles, Lower California. Our year enlistment was expired and here we were discharged and started for home. But, we knew nothing of the whereabouts of our home or friends. I, Levi Savage, arrived in Salt Lake Valley on the 16th day of October 1847. Father and Mathew, my younger brother, had arrived in Salt Lake Valley about three weeks previous to my arrival (having come across the plains with the pioneers). Father brought Jane Mathers to cook for him. I had formed some acquaintance with this Miss Jane Mathers while traveling from the vicinity of Nauvoo to Council Bluff. We renewed our acquaintance and on the 23rd day of January 1848, I married her. On the 11th of January 1851 she gave birth to my first child, a son, whom we named Levi Mathers Savage. Mathers is his mother's maiden name. On the 29th day of December 1851, his mother died, and on the last day of the year she was buried. At the October conference in 1852 I was called with Elders

Ludington, Bly, Dewey, and Chauncy West on a gospel mission to Siam. None of us got there, but Elam Ludington, and he was robbed out there. He then went to China and from there home.

"We sailed from San Francisco to Calcutta and from there to other parts and places. From Calcutta Elam Ludington and I, Levi Savage, sailed to Rangoon, Burma, hoping to cross the country from there to Siam. But, on our arrival in Rangoon we learned the country from there to Siam was a jungle infested with ferocious animals and renegades, which made it unsafe to cross in small companies, so I went to Maulmain, Burma. I stopped with an English man by the name of George Jefferson. I ate at his family table and had a bed and room to myself for a whole year, and he did not charge me a cent. . . . Mr. Lewis, the American Counsul in Calcutta, was very kind in furnishing me a free passage on an American ship from Calcutta to Boston, North America. Satisfactory arrangements now completed, I went on the American ship, 'Herbert,' with Captain Done on the 12th P.M. October 1855."[2]

Levi Savage arrived in Boston in early March. He continued in missionary service in New York and Connecticut until June 16, 1856, when he went to meet a large number of immigrants at Castle Gardens, New York. Two days later he wrote in his diary:

"This morning I commenced to prepare to start for

home in company with about 500 Saints who are in the charge of Elders Willie and Atwood. Elders Willie and Atwood were obliged to stop a few days to attend to some business; consequently, they gave me charge of the Saints until they overtook us. At five o'clock P.M. we set sail up the North River, and at ten P.M. arrived at the depot where we took the cars for Duncurk."

Between this time and July 10, Levi left the Willie company and visited family and friends in Illinois and Ohio. He rejoined the immigrants at Iowa City on July 10 and on July 11 wrote this entry, which includes two familiar phrases in many of Levi's writings (in italics): "Today, *agreeable to council,* I reported myself to Brother Daniel Spencer, the agent for forwarding the Saints. *He requires my assistance, and I commenced.*"[3]

Such was the faithfulness of Levi Savage.

In 1907 William Woodward, who had been a subcaptain in the Willie handcart company fifty years before, attended a reunion of handcart pioneer veterans. Afterward, he wrote down some of his reflections in a letter to Church president Joseph F. Smith, including the following:

"Levi Savage who was censured for his truthful statement at Florence, was I think the best help we had—resolute & determined his whole soul was for the salvation of our company."[4]

The role Levi Savage played in helping preserve the

lives of Willie company members is powerfully portrayed in a scene in *17 Miracles* with the Linford family. The very last of the remaining flour ration was given out on October 19. Levi Savage apparently had saved a portion of that ration to keep himself alive for one more day. The next night, October 20, Levi visited the Linford family. Amasa Linford, 11 years old at the time, later wrote in his father's diary:

"While father was sick and just before he died of starvation, Levi Savage emptied his flour sack to make him some skilly as it was called; after eating this he died."[5]

20

What can you tell us about the scene with the dried-out sea biscuits?

T. C.: The sea biscuits scene represents a near miss that I created in the production of the film when the editor, Tanner, and I cut out this scene because we felt the film had become too long. I wanted to focus the story more. Then we had a screening for a stake in Salt Lake, put together by their president, my friend Ted Adams. We learned from that screening that the thing most viewers liked most about the film was seeing and learning about the miracles. That, plus a prod from Kathy Tanner, my business partner's wife, led us to put the sea biscuits scene back in. I am so grateful that we did. It is a high point for me in the film and a great tribute to Ann Rowley and her descendants, currently estimated to number more than 15,000.

Jolene: Ann Jewell Rowley was a 48-year-old widow when she traveled with her family to Utah with the Willie handcart company. She was the second wife of William Rowley, whose first wife had died. Ann's autobiography also tells of remarkable and well-known events from Church history of which she was a part:

"We had a beautiful home . . . in the Parish of Buckley, Worcestershire, England. We were members of a religious body called the 'United Brethren.'

"Before our first child was born, we were privileged to hear a man named Wilford Woodruff proclaim a new gospel message. We really went to hear this man because we were curious and because we had heard that the Church of England had sent a constable to arrest him, but this man had converted him [the constable] instead. Then the church sent two spies who were commissioned to set in on the meetings and report back. They too were converted, so the church dared not send anyone else. We all wanted to hear this astonishing man.

"We had only to hear him once, and William and I knew with all our hearts that he was offering us a priceless treasure. We accepted his offer and were baptized into the

'Church of Jesus Christ of Latter-day Saints.' All but one of the 600 members of the United Brethren were converted and baptized at the time.

"We dreamed of going to Zion, where we could be with the main body of the Saints, but money was the problem here too. William was never to see Zion . . . he died when Jane was 6 months old [February 14, 1848].

"I was left a widow with 7 children under 12 years of age and the stepchildren of William's first marriage. I was very grateful for the gospel of Jesus Christ and the comfort it gave me. I knew that our parting was only temporary and that viewed from the eternities, this was but a fleeting moment. I also knew that no matter how fleeting a moment it was, I had to make the best of it. I had a very real job to do. The children had to be fed and clothed, but the big task and the one I must accomplish, is to get us all to Zion. I must be among the people of my faith and I must get the temple work done for us. Each person that could earn money at all, was required to work."[1]

Ann's biography gives the family account of the multiplied sea biscuits, which was presented in *17 Miracles:*

"There came a time when there seemed to be no food at all. Some of the men left to hunt buffalo. Night was coming and there was no food for the evening meal. I asked God's help as I always did. I got on my knees, remembering two hard sea biscuits that were still in my trunk. They had been left over from the sea voyage. They were not large, and were so hard they couldn't be broken. Surely, that was not enough to feed 8 people. But 5 loaves and 2 fishes were not enough to feed 5,000 people either, but through a miracle, Jesus had done it. So, with God's help, nothing is impossible. I found the biscuits and put them in a dutch oven and covered them with water and asked for God's blessing. Then I put the lid on the pan and set it on the coals. When I took off the lid a little later, I found the pan filled with food. I kneeled with my family and thanked God for his goodness."[2]

21

Was Betsy Cunningham actually dead when her family buried her in a shallow grave?

T. C.: Whether Betsy Cunningham was dead or only in a state in which her heart rate and breathing had slowed to the point where life was undetectable will never be known. Either way, though, the whole story is a miracle. It was a miracle that the family came back—they didn't just travel a few yards and then turn around and go back. Not until that afternoon did they return to the place where they had left her that morning. It was a miracle that the wolves left her untouched, especially as she was not buried but only covered with sagebrush. No matter what, Betsy Cunningham's life from that day forward was the result of a miracle.

Jolene: Several biographies of various members of the Cunningham family tell of this miracle. They contain minor variations, but all recount essentially the same story of Betsy's miraculous revival. It appears that the first published account of this miracle was in 1947 in *Heart Throbs of the West*, by Kate B. Carter. It reads:

"At one time Elizabeth, the subject of our sketch, was left for dead on the plains, as she was thought to be frozen to death. The ground was frozen so hard that they could not dig a grave so they just wrapped her in a blanket and laid the body on the ground and hurried on to make camp for the night, as darkness was fast overtaking them. After they had reached camp, the mother of Elizabeth felt impressed to go back to the child. Her friends ridiculed the idea, but the mother was determined, for she maintained that the child was not dead. She had been promised in Scotland that if she was faithful, that she and all her family would reach Zion in safety. She went back to the child and found her undisturbed by the wolves. She carried the child back to camp and worked over her. Some hot water was spilt on her foot and it caused a quiver to go through the limb. Convinced that she was still alive, they kept up

Elizabeth "Betsy" Cunningham Kelly (left) and her sister Margaret Cunningham Binnall, about 1920

their efforts until they brought her back to life. This is the Elizabeth who lived to be the mother of thirteen children, and the foster-mother of three others."[1]

Two of Elizabeth's (Betsy's) siblings, George and Margaret, are portrayed in *17 Miracles;* another sister, 18-year-old Catherine, was also with the family.

Betsy's brother, George, was 15 years old at the time of the trek. He later wrote an autobiography that gives further evidence of the faith and spirituality of his family. The following excerpts describe scenes portrayed in the film:

"My parents were the first to embrace the Gospel around our district [in Scotland] but later nearly half of the citizens joined, probably twenty or thirty families. I was raised in the strictest sense of the word 'Mormon.' In the spring of 1856 the chance opened up for us to emigrate to this country, for which we were truly thankful. We sold our small effects and bade our friends farewell, took a train for Glasgow and from there by steamboat to Liverpool. On the 4th of May we embarked on the ship 'Thornton' bound for New York.

"How well I remember the first step I took on American soil! How thrilled I was to be in the land of the free—the land of promise! I had been taught to believe it was the land of promise blessed above all other lands, and although only a boy of fifteen years, I felt like thanking God for the blessing I then enjoyed.

"[Our journey from Iowa City] meant a three-hundred mile trip through the state of Iowa before reaching a permanent starting place at Winter Quarters or Florence, where we arrived after several weeks of pulling, hauling and praying. People sneered at us and laughed, crying out 'Gee-haw' but this did not discourage us in the least. We knew that we were on the right track and that was enough.

"I remember being at a meeting [at Florence] when Brother Levi Savage . . . spoke. He counseled the old and sickly to remain until another spring. The tears rolled down his cheeks as he prophesied that if such took the journey at that late season of the year, their bones would strew the way. At length we started, but the number was greatly reduced, about a hundred remaining. I must state here that there was not one of our [mostly Scottish] hundred [stayed behind] for which we received great praise. The wagons were heavily loaded and we were delayed much by having to wait on them."[2]

Other members of the Willie and Martin handcart companies recorded incidents of family members being brought back from the dead, according to their faith in promises given their families before leaving England. One of those revived in the Martin company was Thomas Bleak, whose father, James Godson Bleak, had served as president of the Whitechapel Branch of the Church in London just before his family emigrated from England. A prophecy given in a meeting promised James that "he and his family shall gather to Zion in safety, and not one of them shall fall by the way."[3] At that time, James and Elizabeth Bleak had four children, ages 1 to 6. Thomas was 4.

At least twice during the trek, James's own life hung in the balance. Through his faith, the ministrations of his wife, and the assistance of fellow travelers Maria Normington and Francis Webster, he was spared. In an article published in the *Juvenile Instructor* in June 1902, James wrote in the third person of his reliance on the promise he had been given and of the miraculous healing of his 4-year-old son, Thomas Nelson Bleak:

"Two good sisters, one an aged widow, the other unmarried, in the kindness of their womanly hearts, had volunteered to assist the mother by taking charge of one of the children at the close of each day's travel till the following morning. The offer was gratefully accepted and the four-and-a-half-year-old, blue-eyed, fair-haired boy, became the chosen one to share the added protection of their tender care.

"One morning, after a very cold night, when winter had overtaken the company, these sisters were horrified to find their little pet lying between them dead, as they decided, and in this condition they brought him to his parents. His father, who had already made a fire, took the child and began by anointing him with consecrated oil, and praying over him, calling upon the Lord to keep His promise that not one of the family should fall by the way in gathering to Zion. Tests were applied, but not a heartbeat or other sign of life was in the child. The father continued to administer, to chafe the limbs and body, and to call upon the Lord to fulfill His promise. After what appeared to the sympathetic fellow travelers and sufferers as a very long time, the father thought he saw a slight flutter in the child's throat; this encouraged further rubbing, chafing and administration until finally, by God's power and blessing, the dear child unclosed his eyes and is now a resident of Salt Lake City, father of nine children and likewise a grandfather.

"That word of the Lord, given by the gift of tongues [in England], inspired a faith, an assurance, which prompted administrations and prayers in behalf of a child who was looked upon as dead by the scores present in that camp; and it is the father's conviction that, if that promise had not been made the boy would have been given up as dead; and would have been laid with the hundreds of that company who were buried by the wayside in that trying journey."[4]

Jason Celaya and Natalie Blackman
portrayed George Padley and Sarah Franks
in 17 Miracles

CONCLUSION

T. C.: *17 Miracles* recounts only a few of the stories associated with the handcart migration. As Jolene has demonstrated, there are many other stories that were not depicted in the film. I believe that many more equally inspiring stories were never documented by those who experienced or witnessed them. But what the surviving record reveals clearly is that those who participated in that epic journey were driven by a faith, diligence, and courage that compel our admiration.

I am grateful to have been able to bring a few of these stories to life and hope that viewers of the film will share my belief that many of the experiences had by these stalwart people are miracles, in that they are not explainable by normal means. As such, they testify of the reality of God and his love for us, his children.

Jolene: Many faithful individuals lost limbs and loved ones to the cold, but they recorded strong testimonies of their continuing devotion to God and his Church.

A favorite quotation comes from William Jones of the Hodgetts wagon company, as recorded by his 19-year-old daughter, Louisa. William died two days after crossing the Platte River on October 19. The Hodgetts company was stranded near the Martin company during that time and suffered the same privations and exposure as they did.

"Father called our family to his wagon and said, 'I have pointed you Zionward and I want you never to turn back. God is in his heaven and all is right with us whether we are in this earth or out of it. God will be with you. If you stumble and fall back, pick yourselves up and go on again.'"[1]

Such is the heritage of faith that belongs not only to the descendants of these pioneers who suffered so much but to all who benefit today from learning about their faith and their sacrifices. May we recognize the sustaining miracles in our own lives and use our own gifts and talents to bless others.

Acknowledgments

T. C.: Writing, producing, and directing *17 Miracles* was an extremely rewarding experience for me. Big thank-yous to my co-producer, Ron Tanner; editor and son, Tanner Christensen, and his cute wife, Carly; my wife, Katy; our daughter, Tess, and members of the makeup department; our wonderful crew that stuck it out through all the long days and bitter cold winter work; and the cast and extras headed up by many descendants of the great people whose stories are told in the film. Thanks also to Sheri Dew, Jana Erickson, Suzanne Brady, and others at Deseret Book for their interest in the film and their help in preparing this book for publication.

Jolene: I am very grateful to T. C. Christensen and Deseret Book for giving me the opportunity to work on this book. I am grateful for untiring cheerleaders among family and friends, particularly Sherryl Fowers. Their interest and support are invaluable. I am especially grateful for my husband, Michael, who allows me the freedom to spend endless hours at the computer and away from home, sharing the stories and sacred testimonies of a special group of friends from 1856.

Notes and Sources

The most accurate and comprehensive book on the Willie and Martin handcart companies currently available is *The Price We Paid: The Extraordinary Story of the Willie & Martin Handcart Pioneers,* by Andrew D. Olsen.

I Walked to Zion: True Stories of Young Pioneers on the Mormon Trail, by Susan Arrington Madsen, is a compact, accessible compilation.

Journey to Zion: Voices from the Mormon Trail, by Carol Cornwall Madsen, is a monumental collection of moving and powerful pioneer writings.

Remember: The Willie and Martin Handcart Companies and Their Rescuers—Past and Present, compiled by members of the Riverton Wyoming Stake, was the first to have published in one volume a comprehensive chronology chart and company journals.

Tragedy and Triumph—Your Guide to the Rescue of the 1856 Willie and Martin Handcart Companies, by Howard K. Bangerter and Cory W. Bangerter, provides a chronology chart, maps, and other information helpful in quickly grasping the overall story. Its small size makes it easy to take along on the trail.

Emigrating Journals of the Willie and Martin Handcart Companies and the Hunt and Hodgetts Wagon Trains, by Lynne Slater Turner, places quotations from pioneers in context with dates and a summary of the story.

The Willie Handcart Company: Their Day-by-Day Experiences, Including Trail Maps and Driving Directions, by Paul D. Lyman, is a valuable resource that includes 89 detailed maps.

Tell My Story, Too, by Jolene Spendlove Allphin, details the stories of many of the 1856 belated handcart pioneers and their known rescuers. It includes 258 biographical sketches and 302 pictures.

QUESTION 3

1. Ten months after the rescue, John Poole married Jane Bitton of the Martin handcart company. He later joked that this was his right because he had rescued her from a snowbank. "The Life History of Jane Bitton Poole," files of Jolene S. Allphin.

QUESTION 4

1. B. Fay Byington, "Elizabeth Crook Panting, Journey from England to Utah," files of Jolene S. Allphin.
2. Byington, "Elizabeth Crook Panting."

QUESTION 5

1. "Autobiography of Agnes Caldwell," typescript of interview conducted by Veara Southworth Fife, Daughters of Utah Pioneers, Salt Lake City, Utah, 2; hereafter cited as Daughters of Utah Pioneers. See also Susan Arrington Madsen, *I Walked to Zion* (Salt Lake City: Deseret Book, 1994), 57–59; Mormon Pioneer Overland Travel Database, 1847–68, The Church of Jesus Christ of Latter-day Saints, http://mormontrail.lds.org; hereafter cited as Mormon Pioneer Overland Travel Database.
2. "Autobiography of Robert Reeder," Daughters of Utah Pioneers. See also *The David Reeder Family History,* compiled by Adolph Madsen Reeder, 2d ed. (North Salt Lake, Utah: DMT Publishing, 2006), 161.
3. Thomas Caldwell, "Short Sketch of Thomas Caldwell," 1–2, files of Jolene S. Allphin.

QUESTION 6

1. Levi Savage, diary, Sept. 25, 1854, vol. 5, p. 15, L. Tom Perry Special Collections, Harold B. Lee Library, Brigham Young

University, Provo, Utah; hereafter cited as L. Tom Perry Special Collections. Images and transcription available online at http://catalog.lib.byu.edu/uhtbin/pcnum/1579986#.

QUESTION 7

1. Joseph B. Elder, *Journals of Joseph B. Elder, 1835–1897, Written by Joseph B. Elder (with Additional Genealogical Notes)*, compiled by Henry T. Elder (privately published, 1978), Apr. 25, 1856, p. 4.
2. Elder, *Journals,* Aug. 10, 1856, p. 18.
3. Elder, *Journals,* July 16, 1856, p. 16.
4. Elder, *Journals,* July 18, 1856, p. 16.
5. Elder, *Journals,* Aug. 5, 1856, p. 17.
6. Levi Savage, diary, Sept. 1, 1856, vol. 7, p. 48, L. Tom Perry Special Collections.
7. Savage, diary, Sept. 3, 1856, vol. 7, p. 49.
8. Elder, *Journals,* undated entry between Aug. 18 and Nov. 8, 1856, p. 19.
9. Elder, *Journals,* undated entry, between Aug. 18 and Nov. 8, 1856, pp. 19–21.

QUESTION 8

1. Laleta Dixon, "History of My Ancestor, William James of the Willey Handcart Co., 1856," typescript in Church History Library, Salt Lake City, Utah; hereafter cited as Church History Library; available online at Mormon Pioneer Overland Travel Database, http://mormontrail.lds.org. See also Carol Cornwall Madsen, *Journey to Zion: Voices from the Mormon Trail* (Salt Lake City: Deseret Book, 1997), 625.
2. "Autobiography of George Cunningham," Mar. 29, 1876, p. 4, files of Jolene S. Allphin. See also *Treasures of Pioneer History,* compiled by Kate B. Carter, 6 vols. (Salt Lake City: Daughters of Utah Pioneers, 1956), 5:252–56; Madsen, *Journey to Zion,* 636; Mormon Pioneer Overland Travel Database, http://mormontrail.lds.org.

3. Joseph B. Elder, *Journals of Joseph B. Elder, 1835–1897, Written by Joseph B. Elder (with Additional Genealogical Notes)*, compiled by Henry T. Elder (privately published, 1978), Aug. 13, 1856, p. 18.
4. "Autobiography of Emily Hill Woodmansee," in *Representative Women of Deseret,* compiled by Augusta Joyce Crocheron (Salt Lake City, 1884), 82–90. See also Leonard J. Arrington Historical Archives, Utah State University, Special Collections, Series 6, Box 10, Folder 3, Item 3.
5. *Hymns of The Church of Jesus Christ of Latter-day Saints* (Salt Lake City: The Church of Jesus Christ of Latter-day Saints, 1985), no. 309.
6. Elder, *Journals,* Aug. 15, 1856, p. 18.
7. Levi Savage, diary, Aug. 15, 1856, vol. 7, p. 45, L. Tom Perry Special Collections,
8. Savage, diary, Aug. 17, 1856, vol. 7, p. 45.

QUESTION 9

1. B. Fay Byington, *The Family History of the Charles Morris Bell Family* (privately published, 1982), 31–33, and interviews with June M. Cranney by Jolene S. Allphin.
2. Reta L. DeLo, "My Grandmother's Journey from England to Utah," 3, Daughters of Utah Pioneers history file for Elizabeth Crook Panting Wilkes Cranney. Three of the Twelve Apostles ordained by Jesus Christ in America after his resurrection were given the same promise as the apostle John was given in Jerusalem before the crucifixion and death of Jesus Christ. See Luke 9:27 and John 21:20–24 in the Bible and 3 Nephi 28 in the Book of Mormon: Another Testament of Jesus Christ.

QUESTION 10

1. *Recollections of Past Days: The Autobiography of Patience Loader Rozsa Archer,* edited by Sandra Ailey Petree (Logan: Utah State University Press, 2006), 79. Available online at http://digitalcommons.usu.edu/usupress_pubs/37.
2. Elizabeth Horrocks Jackson Kingsford, *Leaves from the Life of*

Elizabeth Horrocks Jackson Kingsford (Ogden, Utah, 1908), 12. Images of the journal pages are available online through the catalog of the Church History Library.

3. Quoted in "Autobiography of William Wignall," 3, Daughters of Utah Pioneers. William states: "I will now commence with my wife's history. . . . I here wish to tell of a few manifestations of God to my wife. (As told by my wife)."
4. John Jaques, diary, Oct. 17, 1856, quoted in Stella Jaques Bell, *Life History and Writings of John Jaques* (Rexburg, Idaho: Ricks College Press, 1978), 144.
5. "History of Louisa Mellor Clark," given at Spring Lake, Utah, Mar. 26, 1881; available online at http://www.localhistory.scit.wlv.ac.uk/genealogy/clark/louisaclark.htm.
6. Susan Arrington Madsen, *I Walked to Zion* (Salt Lake City: Deseret Book, 1994), 45–46.
7. Elizabeth Sermon Camm to her children, Mar. 16, 1892, San Francisco, California, typescript in files of Jolene S. Allphin. See also Lynne Slater Turner, *Emigrating Journals of the Willie and Martin Handcart Companies and the Hunt and Hodgetts Wagon Trains* (published privately, 2006), 216; Mormon Pioneer Overland Travel Database, http://mormontrail.lds.org.
8. Sara Yardley, Melba Yardley, and Harriet Anderson Yardley, "History of Eliza Morton Anderson," 3, files of Jolene S. Allphin. See also Bonnie Miller, *The Millers: The Ancestors & Descendants of Louis Thomas Miller and Martha Marinda Andersen,* 2 vols. (privately published, 2010), 1:103.
9. Mary Ann Poole Richardson, "History of Jane Bitton Poole," files of Jolene S. Allphin.
10. Albert Jones diaries, L. Tom Perry Special Collections, MSS 346, Box 1, 35–36, transcribed by Jolene S. Allphin.
11. Albert Jones [reminiscence], "Utah Heroes Who Pulled Their All across the Plains," *Deseret Evening News,* Sept. 1, 1906, 20, available online at Mormon Pioneer Overland Travel Database, http://mormontrail.lds.org.

Question 11

1. "History of Louisa Mellor Clark," given at Spring Lake, Utah, Mar. 26, 1881; available online at http://www.localhistory.scit.wlv.ac.uk/genealogy/clark/louisaclark.htm.
2. "History of Louisa Mellor Clark."
3. "History of Louisa Mellor Clark."
4. "Weather splendid," Willie company journal, Oct. 14, 1856, quoted in Paul D. Lyman, *The Willie Handcart Company: Their Day-by-Day Experiences, Including Trail Maps and Driving Directions* (Provo, Utah: BYU Studies, 2006), 143. "Hot day," Oct. 2, 3, 4, 5, John Jaques, diary, quoted in *Remember: The Willie and Martin Handcart Companies and Their Rescuers—Past and Present,* compiled by members of the Riverton Wyoming Stake (Salt Lake City: Publishers Press, 1997), 18.
5. "History of Louisa Mellor Clark." See also *Our Pioneer Heritage,* compiled by Kate B. Carter, 20 vols. (Salt Lake City: Daughters of Utah Pioneers, 1958–77), 17:306.
6. "History of Louisa Mellor Clark."
7. "History of Louisa Mellor Clark."
8. In Amy Van Cott, *Generations of Websters* (n.p., 1960), 61–62. See also David O. McKay, "Pioneer Women," *Relief Society Magazine,* Jan. 1948, 8.
9. Van Cott, *Generations of Websters,* 50.
10. Van Cott, *Generations of Websters,* 43.

Question 12

1. Jolene Spendlove Allphin, *Tell My Story, Too* (self-published, 2001), 238.

Question 13

1. Interview with Kim McKinnon, summer 1992, Riverton Wyoming Stake files. Excerpts from transcript of interview sent to Jolene S. Allphin, February 9, 2012. Personal interviews with Kathleen Thacker by Jolene S. Allphin confirm that

during Kathleen's inquiries among descendants for the name of Sarah's fiancé, one remembered Sarah Franks Mackay telling her granddaughter Bernice M. Madsen (Kathleen's first cousin twice removed) that his name was George Padley. Subsequent interviews confirmed that other grandchildren also knew of their grandmother's engagement to George Padley.

2. *Remember: The Willie and Martin Handcart Companies and Their Rescuers—Past and Present,* compiled by members of the Riverton Wyoming Stake (Salt Lake City: Publishers Press, 1997), 206.
3. "Biography of Jesse Soar Taylor: Came to Utah in 1856, written by Ethel Taylor Page, His Daughter," 4, files of Jolene S. Allphin. Jesse's biography indicates that the Taylors were housed in the same tent with the Stones family, with whom Sarah Franks was traveling. Research by Jolene S. Allphin has shown a connection in 1856 between LDS merchants in South Africa and Sarah Franks, who was working in a lace factory in Nottingham, England. This research strongly suggests that George Padley was working as a tailor in Nottingham at that same time.
4. "Old Letters: To a Grandson," *Our Pioneer Heritage,* compiled by Kate B. Carter, 20 vols. (Salt Lake City: Daughters of Utah Pioneers, 1958–77), 3:247–49.

Question 14

1. *Descendants of Thomas Mackay—Utah Pioneer, Volume I* (Murray, Utah: Thomas Mackay Family Organization, 1964), 48–59.
2. Bernice M. Madsen, "The Biography of Sarah Franks Mackay," Daughters of Utah Pioneers.
3. "Autobiography of Mary Ann Barton Allen"; available online at http://freepages.genealogy.rootsweb.ancestry.com/~jleatham/maryAnn.htm.
4. William Henry Perkes journal, 1863; available online at Mormon Pioneer Overland Travel Database, http://mormontrail.lds.org.
5. Paul D. Lyman, *The Willie Handcart Company: Their*

Day-by-Day Experiences, Including Trail Maps and Driving Directions (Provo, Utah: BYU Studies, 2006), 128.

6. See Norma B. Ricketts, *The Mormon Battalion: U.S. Army of the West, 1846–1848* (Logan: Utah State University Press, 1996), 312–13.
7. *Journal of Discourses,* 26 vols. (London: Latter-day Saints' Book Depot, 1854–56), 4:134, 136. See also Carter E. Grant, "Robbed by Wolves: A True Story," *Relief Society Magazine,* July 1928, 358–64; *Deseret News Weekly,* Dec. 10, 1856, 317.
8. Gibson Condie Journal, Microfilm of holograph, film no. 0182342, Family History Library, The Church of Jesus Christ of Latter-day Saints, Salt Lake City, Utah, transcribed by Jolene S. Allphin. Gibson Condie participated in the rescue of the Willie and Martin handcart companies and later married Elizabeth Robinson of the Martin company. Gibson is a great-uncle of President Thomas S. Monson.

QUESTION 16

1. Chad M. Orton, "The Martin Handcart Company at the Sweetwater: Another Look," *BYU Studies* 45, no. 3 (2006): 4–37; available online at byustudies.byu.edu.
2. See Stella Jaques Bell, *Life History and Writings of John Jaques, Including a Diary of the Martin Handcart Company* (Rexburg, Idaho: Ricks College Press, 1978).
3. Lloyd Bartholomew, "Brief Sketches from the Life of James Mellor," 47, Daughters of Utah Pioneers, quoted in Andrew D. Olsen, *The Price We Paid: The Extraordinary Story of the Willie & Martin Handcart Pioneers* (Salt Lake City: Deseret Book, 2006), 325.
4. Albert Jones diaries, L. Tom Perry Special Collections, MSS 346, Box 1, 30, transcribed by Jolene S. Allphin.
5. Solomon F. Kimball, "Belated Emigrants of 1856," *Improvement Era,* Feb. 1914, 288.
6. "Six years before this statement was published, the same author reported Brigham Young's words somewhat differently: 'When President Brigham Young heard of this heroic act, he wept like a

child, and declared that this act alone would immortalize them.' Perhaps one explanation for the difference in these accounts is that they were written in 1908 and 1914, more than 50 years after the rescue and 30 years after Brigham Young's death. Regardless of the differences in these statements, what is most important remains undisputed: the heroic service of these rescuers and Brigham Young's feelings of gratitude toward them." Olsen, *Price We Paid,* 360–61. These rescuers have now been immortalized by sculptor Rusty Bowers's heroic statues on the trail near Martin's Cove.

7. Brent Turek, "Clark Allen Huntington, 1831–1896," unpublished manuscript, available online at http://tellmystorytoo.com/pdf/TellMyStoryToo-ClarkAllenHuntington.pdf.
8. Turek, "Clark Allen Huntington, 1831–1896."
9. William Palmer, "She Stood Tall on Her Knees," *Instructor,* July 1956, 196–97.
10. Josiah Rogerson, "Martin's Handcart Company, 1856 [no. 8]," *Salt Lake Herald,* Nov. 24, 1907; available online at Mormon Pioneer Overland Travel Database, http://mormontrail.lds.org.
11. In Amy Van Cott, *Generations of Websters* (n.p., 1960), 61–62. See also David O. McKay, "Pioneer Women," *Relief Society Magazine,* Jan. 1948, 8.

QUESTION 17

1. James G. Willie, missionary diaries, Nov. 25, 1855, typescript in files of Jolene S. Allphin.
2. "Autobiography of George Cunningham," Mar. 29, 1876, p. 9, files of Jolene S. Allphin. See also *Treasures of Pioneer History,* compiled by Kate B. Carter, 6 vols. (Salt Lake City: Daughters of Utah Pioneers, 1956), 5:252–56; Carol Cornwall Madsen, *Journey to Zion: Voices from the Mormon Trail* (Salt Lake City: Deseret Book, 1997), 639.
3. Paul D. Lyman, *The Willie Handcart Company: Their Day-by-Day Experiences, Including Trail Maps and Driving Directions* (Provo, Utah: BYU Studies, 2006), 162–63.
4. Joseph B. Elder, *Journals of Joseph B. Elder, 1835–1897, Written*

by Joseph B. Elder (with Additional Genealogical Notes), compiled by Henry T. Elder (privately published, 1978), Oct. 20, 1856, p. 22.

5. Levi Savage, diary, July 17, 1856, vol. 7, p. 35, L. Tom Perry Special Collections.
6. Mary Hurren Wight [reminiscences], in James G. Willie History; available online at Mormon Pioneer Overland Travel Database, http://mormontrail.lds.org.

QUESTION 18

1. Andrew D. Olsen, *The Price We Paid* (Salt Lake City: Deseret Book, 2006), 297.
2. John William Southwell, Autobiographical sketch, Sept. 28, 1912; excerpt available online at Mormon Pioneer Overland Travel Database, http://mormontrail.lds.org.
3. "On the Trail with James Godson Bleak, February 1854–February 1860: James Godson Bleak Personal Journal from Feb. 1854 to Feb. 1860," typescript, 17, files of Jolene S. Allphin. While in Martin's Cove, on November 5, 1856, Bleak made a journal entry about the severe reduction of flour rations that day and commented: "Through the blessing of our Father we felt as contented as when we had 1 lb. per head." Bleak's original diary is in the Church History Library.
4. "Samuel Openshaw Diary"; available online at Mormon Pioneer Overland Travel Database, http://mormontrail.lds.org. See also Carol Cornwall Madsen, *Journey to Zion: Voices from the Mormon Trail* (Salt Lake City: Deseret Book, 1997), 648–49.
5. "Biography and Journal of William Lawrence S. [Spicer] Binder," copied from original on Aug. 13, 1947, Daughters of Utah Pioneers, 16.
6. Jaques, diary, Sept. 12, 1856, quoted in Stella Jaques Bell, *Life History and Writings of John Jaques, Including a Diary of the Martin Handcart Company* (Rexburg, Idaho: Ricks College Press, 1978), 135.

7. Jaques, diary, Jan. 8, 1856, quoted in Bell, *Life History and Writings of John Jaques,* 52.
8. Kathryn Mortensen Harmer, *Zion Bound: The Ancestry & Descendants of Arlington Peter & Fannie Burnham Mortensen* (1998), 11–28; Ron Ray, *The Crossing: Trials of 1856* (n.p., 1997), 13–14; *The Morten P. Mortensen Family,* edited by Viva Cluff Whetten and Lillian Jones Richins (1995), 1–22; copies of handwritten histories by Mette Mortensen Rasmussen in files of Jolene S. Allphin,
9. "Journal of Robert Campbell Kirkwood," typescript in files of Jolene S. Allphin; "A Veteran Passes Away," *Deseret Daily News,* July 6, 1893, Church History Library; interviews with Kirkwood descendants by Jolene S. Allphin.
10. Charlotte Mee Beal, "Life Sketch of Charlotte Mee Beal," Daughters of Utah Pioneers.

Question 19

1. Norma Baldwin Ricketts, *The Mormon Battalion, U.S. Army of the West, 1846–1848* (Logan: Utah State University Press, 1996), 177.
2. *Levi Savage Jr. Journal,* compiled by Lynn M. Hilton (Salt Lake City: John Savage Family Organization, 1966), xi–xiii.
3. Levi Savage, diary, July 11, 1856, vol. 7, p. 33, L. Tom Perry Special Collections.
4. Woodward to Smith, Utah State Historical Society Cache Valley Chapter, Cache Valley, Utah-Idaho, 1966–56, reel 5, item 1ab.
5. Golden C. Linford, *Linford Family Heritage* (Rexburg, Idaho: Ricks College Press, 1995), 433–36. John Linford's original diary is in the Church History Library.

Question 20

1. "Autobiography of Ann Jewell Rowley," http://aprilsancestry.com/RowleyWilliam.html. That the members of the Rowley family were united in their 16-year task of getting themselves "all to Zion" was surely a factor in their continuing ability to face pioneering challenges once they arrived in Utah. See *Rowley*

Family Histories: Treasures of Truth from the Lives of William and Ann Jewell Rowley and Their Children, 1835–1930, compiled by Frank Richardson (Salt Lake City, Utah: William & Ann Jewell Rowley Family, 1992).

2. "Autobiography of Ann Jewell Rowley," http://aprilsancestry .com/RowleyWilliam.html.

QUESTION 21

1. *Heart Throbs of the West,* compiled by Kate B. Carter (Salt Lake City: Daughters of Utah Pioneers, 1947), 1:86. See Olive Dunn Binnall, "Biographical Sketch of the Life of Elizabeth Cunningham Kelly," 1930, MSS SC 3312, L. Tom Perry Special Collections. Olive was 36 years old when her grandmother died, and Olive wrote this history 6 years later. That both she and her grandmother lived in American Fork, Utah, adds a further degree of reliability to this account. See also Dale W. Adams, *True Grit: The Elizabeth Cunningham Story* (Park City, Utah, 2006), 11–12; www.manxmormons.com/williamkelly.pdf, 9.
2. "Autobiography of George Cunningham," Mar. 29, 1876, p. 4, files of Jolene S. Allphin. See also *Treasures of Pioneer History,* compiled by Kate B. Carter, 6 vols. (Salt Lake City: Daughters of Utah Pioneers, 1956), 5:252–56. Coincidentally, Elizabeth Panting and her children were in the group that included the Cunningham family. The captain of this hundred was William Woodward.
3. "Two Stories of Handcart Pioneers: James Godson Bleak and Samuel Stucki and Their Wives Elizabeth Moore and Magdalena Stettler," compiled by Ruth Holston Stucki, 4–5, in files of Jolene S. Allphin.
4. Scribo (pseudonym of James Bleak), "An Item of Handcart Experience," *Juvenile Instructor,* June 15, 1902, 365–67.

CONCLUSION

1. In Ron Ray, *The Crossing: Trials of 1856* (n.p., 1997), 78.